The Tao of Nookomis

The Tao of Nookomis

Thomas D. Peacock

ISBN: 978-165-284-8103

This is a work of fiction. Names, characters, places, and incidents are the products of the author's imagination or are used fictitiously. Any resemblance to actual events or persons, living or dead, is entirely coincidental.

First edition: May 2016
Second edition: January 2020

Printed in the United States of America.

To Betsy

Contents

The Tao of Nookomis

*E*ver since I sobered up and decided to go to school, my whole world has changed for the better because, before that, I think I was either giiwashkwebii *(drunk) or had a buzz going, or was hungover, or planning to go on a drunk. It's all kind of a big fog now, anyway. I have to say that I give my ninety-five-year-old great-grandma Nooko (Nookomis, grandmother) much of the credit for my being sober because she sat me down and had that talk when I was ready to listen. A lot of people had that kind of talk with me when I was messed up, but I wasn't ready to listen, or whatever, but it seems like when my great-grandma sat me down it had weight to it, like a big chunk of greasy fry bread with peanut butter and jam on it. Hard to chew, harder to swallow, but really, really good. I remember clear as a bell it went something like this:*

"When I look at you," she began, "I see myself. And now especially when I see you suffering the way you are, I suffer, too. See, I've been there, too. I was you. So when you look at me and the way I've lived my life—an old lady that some people come to for advice, for knowledge, maybe for those skills at beading or making outfits, or the language, or whatever, respected, that's how I feel more than anything—this is what is possible in you, and so much more.

"We are the same. And our hearts match."

And I remember when she said that I got a big lump in my throat, and I was trying to keep it all in, and I finally gave in to it all and rested my head in her lap like when I was a little girl and she would run her fingers through my hair and sing me those old songs in Ojibwe that no one knows anymore except her. And I just let big tears run down my face, and she wiped them away with her frail and knurled hands, and then I looked up and saw she was also in tears.

"Baby girl . . ." she said.

So, anyway, after that day almost two years ago this August, I sobered up. It was hard, I remember, and each day can still be a struggle sometimes. I was able to get checked into Mishomis *(grandfather) House in Red Cliff and got spun dry, as we rezzers sometimes put it. And after my thirty-day inpatient treatment I was given a sponsor and have been attending AA regularly at the elder center.*

Each day since I stopped, I learn something new, not just about things around me but also about myself. And it took a while after I sobered up for my brain to clear up and allow me to even think straight, but eventually I started to think more of what I wanted to do with my life rather than where my next drink was coming from. And I knew I had to go to college if I was going to amount to anything, so that's what I did. So, anyway, this semester I've been taking a class in oral indigenous history at Northland College in Ashland, and the instructor gave us a term project to interview an elder and get their life story, "before it's too late," as he put it.

So, on the way back from class one day, I spun into the assisted living place in Washburn where Grandma Nooko lives now, ever since she fell and broke her hip and couldn't take care of herself anymore because she has been confined to a wheelchair. And I had enough sense to bring me some of that asemaa *(tobacco) to offer her for that knowledge, and I asked her if she would tell me her story.*

Anyway, at first it seemed like she was going to say no, and I got kind of nervous because she didn't say anything for what felt like the longest time, then she finally answered me.

"But I'm not Native, my girl. You know that," she reminded me. "Maybe you need to interview someone else. Me, I'm 150 percent Irish, maybe more."

She laughed just slightly when she said that, then all expression left her face, and she just looked me right in the eyes and didn't say a peep while I thought about how to respond.

"But, Great-Grandma, you know more than anyone as far as I'm concerned. You may not be Ojibwe, but you've lived your whole life out on the rez. You could write a book about us and call it Diary of a 150% Irish Captive, ho wah," *and that got us both laughing.*

I suppose injecting that little bit of rez humor softened her up because she had that same survival humor a lot of us rezzers possess in order to live here and not go crazy because it seems our lives are constantly being bombarded with bad stuff happening, and many of us have had to live though some pretty rugged experiences.

"So, namadabin *(sit down), then," she said and pointed with her lips to the chair next to her bed.*

"Bizindun, Andonis (listen, my daughter), while this mindamooyay chimookomon equay *(old lady white woman) tells you her story."*

She laughed quietly then, and I will always remember her eyes were filled with love. I could easily see that, but now that

I know her story, there were other things as well there—trep-
idation, longing, sadness, fear—a whole lifetime of emotions
all in that one look.

And so the story began, and she told me all the things I had
always wanted to know about her and so much more, a sacred
story. Nowadays I always have a pinch of asemaa *in my hand*
when I share it. Here goes.

I'M GOING TO TELL YOU things, and some of it I've never
shared with anyone before. This is hard for me, and
maybe there will be parts that might make you feel
uncomfortable, but I hope not. I'm just human like
everyone else, a mix of good and the other.

Have you ever read the *Tao*?

That one just caught me out of nowhere. The Tao*? What*
in all hell was my ninety-five-year-old great-grandmother
doing talking about the Tao*? But I wasn't going to let her*
think I was shocked or surprised, so I pretended I was all calm
and shit.

You know, Grandma, I've heard of it, but I don't really
know much about it. I think it is eastern, like Chinese or
something.

A long time ago when I was young and stupid, someone gave me the book *Tao Te Ching* by Lao Tzu. Tzu was
the keeper of the Imperial library in ancient China. Anyway, this person told me to read it, and then we would talk
about it a few parts at a time. The *Tao* is about a lot of
things, I suppose, and each of us could interpret its
mean-ing in our own way, but I've always considered it to
be lessons

on a way of being. Before my eyesight started to fail I always kept a copy of it at my bedside, and I'd read my favorite parts again and again over the years because I think it sums up the way I think about a lot of things, and maybe about the way we humans need help to guide us along the paths we travel in our lives.

Like I said, the *Tao* is about a lot of things, but one of the things the *Tao* speaks to is that each of us are both yin (shadow side) and yang (sun side), all parts that form the whole. None of us is just one side. It says,

When people see things as beautiful,
ugliness is created.
When people see things as good,
evil is created.
Being and non-being produce each other.
Difficult and easy complement each other.
Long and short define each other.
High and low oppose each other.
Fore and aft follow each other.

And I say this because it relates to the story I am going to tell you. My story is both—yin and yang. I am both. I suppose now that I'm old and don't have much time left on this earth I have the need to talk about the past. Otherwise the story will disappear with me.

My late husband, your great-granddad, who you never got to know because he died long before you were even a twinkle, sometimes reminded me I wasn't Indi'n when he had a bit too much of the drink. So I think as much as you've known about me until now is that I came here as a little girl and was adopted and brought up Indi'n. Well, I suppose that's true, I mean, that about sums it up in a single sentence; however, I'm going to fill you in some of the rest, ninety-five years worth. Most of what I have to say will be new to you. And I won't tell you the whole story in one sitting. Maybe you can come back as long as it takes. Today, however, I'm just going to talk it through, straightaway, and then later we'll fill in all the parts of the puzzle that is me.

I could as well have been born on the moon and never met my great-grandmother when she started telling about being born in Ireland.

I was born in County Clare, Shannon, Ireland, in 1920, named Genevieve Mae Bandle. I didn't know myself where in Ireland I was from until I was twenty-one years old, and found out only after writing countless letters and visiting the Children's Aid Society in New York time after time until they finally relented and gave me the information.

I don't know why, but I knew you were Irish. But I didn't know you were born there. I want to ask you so much more about that, a lot more. You've been to New York?

Of course, I *lived* in New York for two years after I graduated from high school. That's later, though.

And when she said that I was thinking, my God, I have never been to New York. My great-grandmother has lived in New York. I never even knew she had left Bayfield County, Wisconsin.

Why have you never mentioned this before?

You never asked me before today.

I want to know everything about you and New York.

Bizaan (quiet), my Genevieve, later.

Sometimes she called me by my given name, Genevieve. I was named after her, after all.

My great-grandmother had a faraway look in her eyes, and they shifted back and forth like she was nervous. I could tell she felt conflicted. There was a lot of pain there, too. I know this now. Maybe with anyone else I would have pressed the subject because I've learned that sometimes we Indians need to be pushy to survive in a white man's world. However, this was my Grandma Nooko and she was old and frail and I loved her deeply, and so I changed the subject.

I was thinking how many of us get so self-consumed we don't even take the time to really know about others. I was so embarrassed I had never taken the time to know my great-grandmother. Now here she was, living in a nursing home somewhere out in the bush in northern Wisconsin, thousands of miles from the land of her birth. So I said to her, Grandma, I never knew you were born in Ireland. I just never knew. I'm so sorry I never took the time to ask you this before.

Grandma Nooko, tell me what you remember about Ireland?

Ireland?

The word sprung from her lips like it was being sung.

Well, Ireland. The thing that comes to mind is that I remember being hungry, and I know now that was reason number one we made the crossing and how I ended up here in northern Wisconsin. Maybe you know what hunger is, but what I'm trying to describe is different. You know nowadays when we say we are starving, but we really aren't, we're just hungry? Well, what I remember was this kind of hunger was different because there really wasn't anything or very, very little to eat, and I remember having to share a couple of boiled potatoes for dinner among the lot of us, then the next day my mother would fry up the peelings for lunch. I suppose you could say we were starving, although when you really are, maybe it's too difficult to face head-on, so we simply call it hungry.

Now think about that, if we hadn't been hungry. Then maybe I would still be there today in County Clare, Shannon, Ireland. Think about how fate plays its role in the paths of our journey in this life. We come to a place along the road and maybe circumstances, say hunger, led us down a different path. So we go down that path, and it forever changes the direction of our lives. So because of fate, or whatever it may be, my feet have never again touched Irish soil. So there is fate and circumstances, and being at a certain place at a certain time, and luck, and timing, and maybe divine intervention. And all of these things play a role in the paths we walk and the people we meet.

Sometimes I've dreamed of what it would be like to see Ireland again. I've seen it in books, *National Geographic*, and watching that Discovery Channel, so I have some idea. When I see those pictures or videos, however, I always have a sense of loss, sadness, like that piece of me is missing. I can't, no, I have never dwelt on it. It's just there, you know, sometimes.

And when she said that, her hand went to her heart.

Great-grandma, you remember a couple of years ago when I came to see you and you had that talk to me about my drinking? I came to see you that day to borrow money from you so I could get more to drink, and I was ready to steal it from you if I had to when you looked the other way, or took your nap. But I didn't. And if you wouldn't have talked to me about my drinking, or I wasn't ready to listen, or if I hadn't showed up that day, or if I did get booze money from you one way or another. I see what you mean about fate and timing, and luck, circumstances, and divine intervention, or whatever.

By all rights I should be dead, Great-grandma. The way I lived and all.

Great-grandma. Ireland? I can't even imagine being stripped of this place, removed from it, this land, the big lake, the islands. This place is so special to me, to us, so sacred. Madeline Island out there in the lake is the center of the Ojibwe universe, the place of our beginning.

Tears came to my eyes just then. And I saw the same, albeit tiny ones, in the corners of hers, eyes that had never seen her homeland in nearly ninety years.

Aye, Ireland, she said. She added the accent, as well.

And that single word, Ireland, carried in it whole stories, dreams, songs.

Great-grandma, tell me what you remember about your mom and dad.

I don't remember my mother's face or voice. In my dreams, however, she is beautiful, and her voice was soft and sometimes now when I watch a television program and one of the female characters is Irish I have this far, distant memory of my mother's voice.

In my dreams she looks like you. Even though you're Indi'n and she was Irish.

You have her eyes and her heart.

I know there was love there. My mother, you know. But it has been so long ago and I was just a little girl.

I remember, vaguely, we were on a ship. And everywhere there were people and some were very ill. And I remember my mother became one of them, sick. I don't know, or remember, maybe they had an infirmary onboard but I remember her lying in a bed, and my father and brother—I had an older brother—we all were there.

A brother? I want to know about your brother, your father as well.

Bizaan, she said. Later.

I don't remember much about my mother and what happened. Only much later, when I was an adult, did I find out she died during the crossing. A lot of people died during the crossings, I understand that now.

Great-grandma, I'm so sorry. I couldn't even imagine losing my mother at such an early age.

Well, that was a long, long time ago, wasn't it? She smiled and laughed slightly. But there was that certain way she used humor to distract herself away from the pain, something many Native people recognize within our circles, where sadness and happiness exist on the same plane. Where laughter and pain share the same breath, the same air.

Sadness, laughter, yin and yang, each forming a whole. She continued.

I forgive her. I think I could not forgive her for a long time. Maybe I needed to forgive myself first, to accept her death.

What do you mean, forgive yourself?

Later, my girl.

Sometimes I think I may confuse my dreams, imaginings, and memory in order to fill in all the gaps of my life. There is a lot of missing, I suppose. I remember when New York came into view, we all stood out on deck and some people were cheering, others crying. My father put me on his shoulders when we first saw the outline of the city in the distance. Both my brother and father, if I hadn't gotten their names from the Catholic Aid Society when I was older, I'd have never known because then I was too young to remember. As it turns out, my brother's name was John and he was ten years old at the time. If he is still alive today he would be ninety-nine years of age. I don't know if he is still around or not because I never was able to find out anything about him, no matter how hard I searched, no matter how many questions I asked.

It is one of those things I have always wondered about, to have a brother out there, somewhere, and then he disappears out of my life.

My girl, life is filled with unanswered questions, and I need to wait until I pass over, I guess, to meet up with him again. I will see him again. In my dreams I come to a river, and he is there on the other side, along with both my Irish and Ojibwe mothers and Irish father, and they are calling my name and telling me to make the final crossing. Sometimes in my dreams there is an actual river there, but at other times it is a river of stars, the Milky Way. Either way, I can see them, there in my dreams.

So I know that someday I will again see my brother John. I've been waiting to do so the entirety of my life. And I don't know what he will look or be like, or whether he will be a child or adult or elderly like me, I just know I will recognize him, and him, me. He will say, "Sister," and when I hear the word I will run to him.

And I was thinking when she spoke of her brother that I now know I had a great-uncle named John, who was from Ireland, who I will also meet someday, who will be waiting for me on the other side of a river of water, or of stars. And I reached out and took my great-grandmother's hand in mine.

My father. His name was Clarence Bandle. I have to tell you that, for many years, all I felt toward him was anger. Anger because of what he did or didn't do. You see, when we were finally allowed off ship in New York to begin our new life, we didn't have anywhere to live, and he had to get a job right away, and we moved into a rooming house crowded with many other families. I just know that it was dirty and old and there were a lot of others living there. There wasn't enough to eat, and it was cold, and my brother and I spent a lot of time out on the streets. And maybe my father was grieving for my mother, or maybe he was overwhelmed with the responsibility of trying to raise two children alone, or maybe he took to the drink, or maybe he couldn't accept the responsibility of caring for us on his own. Whatever it was I will probably never know, but he eventually took me to the Children's Aid Society and left me there one day, and he told me he would be back to get me when things got better. In my dreams he promised me that.

But I never saw him again. I still remember that day, clearly, as if it were yesterday. And now I'm ninety-five years old, and I've been waiting for him for nearly my entire lifetime.

Her voice was breaking, but she was doing her best to contain herself, so mostly she was strong, her jaw set firmly, eyes looking straight ahead. She continued.

Like I said, I couldn't reconcile why he did this for many, many years, so I carried all of this anger, here, in my heart, toward him.

Have you forgiven him?

Yes. Yes, I have.

Listen to me now when I say this. You see, I realize I will never know in my lifetime what was in his heart the day he left me with the Aid Society. And I won't know until I meet him again on the other side, and it won't even matter then because when we cross to the other side the overwhelming emotion we feel will be love. I believe that. Anger, resentment, jealousy—all of those things that weigh on us here in our earthly home will be no more. So I knew I had to forgive myself first for being angry with him before I could forgive him. Anger, I've realized through living, is mostly wasted energy—it smolders there in the one who is angry, eating away at them. And too often the person at whom the anger is directed is not really affected. So the only one who is destroyed by the anger is the one carrying it in their heart.

When I was finally able to locate information about my father, I found out that he died in 1936 in New York, a few years before I moved there. I don't know the circumstances, or where he was buried. I don't know if he did the same to my brother John, left him with the Aid Society, or if he raised him, or if my brother went off on his own. I don't know these things. I think if I were ever to find his grave now, I would probably ask him, in a respectful way, about these things, about why he left me with the Aid Society, why he never came back for me. This is what I would say: "I have forgiven myself for the anger I once had for you. I forgive you as well."

Such is the way of life, my Genevieve. I still love him. He was my father, after all. Anger, love, forgiveness, we are all of these things, yin, yang.

We need to learn to forgive.

I began to weep when she said that. I am just a big crybaby sometimes, guess I've always been like that. Can't help it. I don't know, but I guess maybe all of the wrongs committed against me in my life all appeared like a big movie screen in my head all at the same time, and then I saw each of them one by one, and I knew I still carried resentments—of people and circumstances, of poor choices and decisions. Anger toward my own father, who drank hard and beat my mother when he was all liquored up and snaky, who left us to fend for ourselves so he could drink some more. Anger for my mother, who put up with his shit for too long. Anger toward teachers at that high school in Bayfield who treated me like some kind of loser and let me know without even mouthing it that I wasn't going to amount to jack shit. Anger toward myself for drinking years away of my life, for having sex with drunken, drugged-up men just so I could have a place to crash, or for something to eat, or more to drink, or to get high. Anger for giving my mother years of grief, for making her wonder night after night, days, months, whether I was even alive. And I could only hope that maybe one day I might come to a place along the road of my life where I will be able to cast each of my angers, resentments, and regrets away.

Maybe be more like Grandma Nooko, to be able to forgive myself, to forgive others. And maybe I could do it before I was like ninety-five years old.

So, because I was still young and stupid, and still carried resentments and anger, I said, I think if I were you, I wouldn't be able to forgive my father.

Forgiveness begins by forgiving oneself.

I love you so much, she said, holding me like she did when I was a little girl and feeling lost and alone, angry.

Accept, she said. Accept that sometimes there are no answers.

The hard things we face in this life are not always lessons to be learned, she reminded me. Sometimes things just happen.

When I recovered, I returned to my questions.

Grandma, what happened at the Children's Aid Society?

I was there for a while. I don't know how long. I just remember the place was filled with other children, and it was noisy, and we slept on cots in long rows and the blankets were scratchy, and there were these nuns who cut off all of us girls' hair so we wouldn't be passing around nits, and they made us wear clothes that were too big for us. And we took baths with lye soap made there by the nuns, and they made us use scrub brushes all over our bodies.

Have you heard of the orphan trains? I was one of the young ones put on those trains. I don't remember what the circumstances were, but one day they told me I was going to be put on a train and that it would take me to a new home, and that I would find a new mother and father. And I said no, I have a mother and father. I don't want or need to go anywhere. But I went anyway because I was only six years old and didn't have any choice. The train was filled with children, matrons, and a few of the nuns, and we rode for what seemed like days and days, sleeping on the train, and at every stop a matron would have us change into our Sunday clothes and march us out onto the platform and have us stand perfectly still, and tell us to act our best. There would be couples who would meet the train at each of the stops, all kinds of different people—farmers, clergy, business people, people who looked like they had money, people who looked like they didn't have a dime—all sorts. And they would pick out children, like we were cattle or pets, and the chosen would go away with them.

And eventually, after many days, there was a man and woman who chose me. That was in 1926, Ashland, Wisconsin, and they introduced themselves as Mr. and Mrs. Belanger. Their first names were Donald and *Zozed* and they became my new mother and father, your great-great-grandfather and grandmother. He was a white man and she was a full-blood Indi'n, Ojibwe. I don't know if they could have chosen me if they both were Indi'n. Just knowing how things were then, I suspect that the man had to be white because they were the ones with the rights.

I remember being frightened of them at first, but I had no choice. The woman who would become my new mother took me by the hand, and we walked through the depot out to the lot to where their car was parked. Don't ask me how but I knew she was Indi'n then and there. Maybe I had heard stories about wild Injuns somewhere, and that only made me fear more, that's for sure.

Wild Injuns, we both said at nearly the same time, and then we were both laughing because we knew the word, and all the pain it has caused in our communities over the years, to be regarded as nothing more than animals, to be denigrated and dehumanized and treated like that. To end up even calling each other that name and all the others, to accept the labels put on us, to believe all of the lies—drunken Injuns, wild Injuns, lazy Injuns, wagon burners, and more. And now, to laugh because it hurt so much for so long that laughing seemed the only sensible thing to do.

I'm laughing. My Grandma thinks I'm a wild Injun, I said again, laughing. Well, I kinda, sorta used to be one of 'em, but I'm on the straight and narrow now, kinda, sorta.

Like I said, my great-grandmother has the same survival humor as many of us rez Indians. We laughed until we spent ourselves of it. Then I returned to my questions.

Grandma Nooko, you talked about fate and luck, circumstances, being at the right (or wrong) place at the right (or wrong) time, and divine intervention. Have you made sense of coming to the reservation, of being adopted, and of spending most of your life here, being brought up Ojibwe, so much so that most people don't even consider you to be anything but Native?

I guess I've thought about it, even more so as I've gotten older. I guess you would say I'm very fortunate—fortunate to have been chosen by my new mother and to be raised by her, to be loved by her, to have lived nearly the entirety of my lifetime in this special place. The people of this place accepted me completely, without reservations (no pun intended) aaayyy . . .

Aaayyy, that always makes us Indi'ns laugh. Whenever it is said, it is accompanied by laughter.

If I hadn't come here, I wouldn't have married the man I married, or had my two daughters, or loved their children as my grandchildren, or been part of this sacred place, or had you as my Genevieve. I can't imagine living my life any other way.

If I were to have had a choice, I would walk no other path but this one.

I was chosen to be here.

All 150 percent of you, I said, and we laughed again. Then I asked her:

Tell me a little bit about growing up in Red Cliff. I want to come back, of course, and interview you in much more depth about all the parts of your life—about Ireland, New York, the orphan train—to get as many details as I can. I know you have a lot more stories about each of those parts of your life, but for now, today, maybe tell me what you take away the most from growing up here on the rez.

You know, there weren't a lot of other kids when I first came here. What we know now because we finally have our history is that the government had taken most of them and put them into those boarding or mission schools. All of the children I would meet later, my cousins and friends, had been taken. So sometimes I wonder if that wasn't one of the reasons my mother selected me from the orphan train. Maybe she missed having a child at home and I filled that void.

Can you imagine, having to send your own children away and not being able to see them for years? Can you imagine having to walk your child to a bus, and then watch it pull out and disappear down the road, knowing it was not going to return at the end of the day, or maybe even the end of the year, and year after year goes by, and when they return they are nearly adults. Can you imagine the heartbreak of that?

And just then I thought of when I was fifteen years old and pregnant, and how when I told my mother she looked so terribly disappointed because she, too, had gotten pregnant at fifteen but had chosen to raise her baby, me, and how I knew then I couldn't have a baby then because I was just a child myself, and how she took me to Planned Parenthood in Superior where I had an abortion, and how we kept it our secret, and how on the way home my mother pulled the car off the side of Highway 13 where there was an opening along Lake Superior, how she put her hands to her face and wept, and she said she didn't blame me.

I don't blame you, my girl, she said.

What are you thinking, Genevieve? You look sad and far away.

I was thinking of what it would be like to give your child away, I said, a lie, a half-truth. I have never told my great-grandmother the story of when I was fifteen.

Grandma Nooko, I began. I was going to finally tell her. But before I could say a thing, she continued, and so my secret remained with me.

Just for a while longer.

So I grew up Indi'n, I guess you could say. My mother *Zozed* taught me to speak fluent Ojibwe, and I suppose every once in a while some of the real Indi'ns in Red Cliff were jealous because I was given that knowledge, but really, it wasn't their fault they couldn't speak it. They had it ripped from them in those schools where they were sent. They told me the stories about what it was like there, of being hit with rulers, and having to kneel on hard peas, and who knows what else for speaking the language. They told me of running away when they could no longer contain their loneliness, of walking the rails back toward their homes, of stealing food and water where they could. Of finally being caught and taken back to school. Of being put into a room without windows and kept in it for days, where they were fed only bread and water.

No, I never considered myself any better because I was fortunate to be among language speakers and other knowledgeable people, the stories and songs. My mother, *Zozed*, took me to the ceremonies that were illegal back then, ceremonies the priest at the church would surely have banned. So I got to be around all of that.

And the same thing is true about learning beading and making outfits. Mother *Zozed* taught me how to sew and do appliqué beadwork, and work deer hides. So I learned it all from her—how to make dance outfits, shawls, ribbon shirts, breechcloths, yokes, and moccasins. And I've used those skills until my eyes and hands gave out to make a little extra income, and to give back, as well, because I gave a lot of it away. When the pow-wow committee came to me some years back, I beaded the tiara the Red Cliff princess wears every year. I made the moccasins for many of the dancers you see today at the Fourth of July pow-wow. And when they needed someone to teach the language in Headstart, I was the language grandma, teaching what I could to our littlest ones.

I only recall a few times when I was reminded in a disrespectful way that I am not really from here, that I am non-Native. Some years back one of the elderly ladies at ENP (Elderly Nutrition Program) said something that maybe I shouldn't be the one teaching language because I'm *chimookomon* (Caucasian, long knife). That lady didn't know the language herself, of course, and I know it was not her fault, so what she said I couldn't hang onto. I remember I was angry for just an instant, but I was able to hide it as best I could, and responded only that I thought she was homely as sin, in Ojibwe, of course. I said, well, I may be non-Native, but you, you're homely as sin, girl.

We laughed. Nooko could be so funny sometimes. Several homely women in Red Cliff village appeared in my mind, and I'm sure one of them was the one she was referring to.

I think, however, the one time that still sometimes bothers me was when that Bear fellow on the tribal council tried to pull my lease because he said we should only be giving land leases to tribal members. I'd lived on that lease land for over forty years and even after my husband, who

20

was a tribal member, died, I had no problem getting the lease renewed each year. The council had promised I would be able to live there until I died. That Bear's motion was eventually defeated, but it was a reminder to me that small minds are everywhere, and they do things that can bring tremendous damage to individuals. What was even more ironic was that he was my husband's nephew.

I had almost forgotten about the land lease issue. I was thinking I was too young to vote when that happened. That fat bastard was still on the council. Every time I recalled what he tried to do I wanted to march down to the tribal center and punch him right in the face.

But my great-grandma, she had yet another lesson to teach me. Not by telling me what I should do, or how I should act toward others, but in the way she lived.

I harbor no ill will toward him. He has a lot of health problems, diabetes, and is in a wheelchair now. I feel for him. His mother and I were friends. She was kind. Maybe he didn't learn kindness and the other things he should have learned. Maybe in life he hadn't yet been humbled, because I know sometimes we have more empathy toward others only when we ourselves have been disrespected, humiliated, ostracized, or otherwise mistreated. I don't know. It's not for me to judge. I just know that everything is in a circle, that we sometimes reap what we sow.

Great-grandma, I still can't believe that anyone could do something so mean. I get so frustrated with people like that. They seem to be everywhere, and some of them are our own Native people. They just cause all this mayhem and don't even consider the hurt it is causing others.

And when I said that, I thought of something just a few years earlier when I was in the local VFW all liquored up and

Bear was sitting at the other end of the bar. I looked up at him when I saw him there, and gave him a sneer, and I mumbled something like "What you looking at, you fat SOB" under my breath, and how I was sure he heard me, but didn't say anything, just looked over at me and my tits, that pervert son of a bitch who's old enough to be my daddy. And I wanted to tell that to my Grandma Nooko but didn't see it as going anywhere, so I didn't say a peep. I continued with my questions.

I want to interview you separately about my great-grandfather and how you met, and about your children, especially my grandmother. I know that particular talk is going to take a lot of time. Is it okay for me to come back to that? I just think that part of your life deserves its own attention.

I will tell you more, then, about my mother, what I remember. My husband, God rest his soul, was a good man, and we raised two wonderful daughters, both of whom have since passed on. Your grandmother was my youngest. She was full of piss and vinegar. I outlived them all, and that is hard. To bury a spouse is difficult enough but to do the same to your own children is painful beyond definition, even though they both lived until they were nearly seventy years old. They were still my little girls, no matter how old. So, yes, we'll come back to that. Their stories are deserving of more attention.

I had noticed, of course, that Nooko had not mentioned her adoptive father, the white man, and probably the only reason the church would have approved giving an orphan child to a reservation family in the first place. And I knew I had to ask, so it just kind of blurted out.

Grandma Nooko, I notice you haven't mentioned your adoptive father much at all. What was he like?

He was a rotten son of a bitch, she said.

And . . . ? I pried. After all, I'm a mixed-blood Ojibwe and have enough of that pushy white blood in me to ask.

Nooko just sat there for what seemed like the longest time, and I could tell she really didn't want to say anything. And it got so quiet the cheap Walmart clock on the wall was the only sound in the room. And my Nooko, I don't know, I didn't want to have her talk about anything that might upset her, and I could see she was visibly upset, so I just took one of her hands while her other hand fetched a handkerchief from the night-gown she was wearing, and she wiped moisture that had gathered just under her nose.

Grandma, I'm so sorry. Please, let's just talk about something else.

But then she just said it.

He used to come to my room.

Great-grandma, please. I'm so sorry. Please. I'm so sorry to have brought it up and to upset you like this.

But she just looked me in the eyes, and I could tell she was resolute.

No, she said. I wanted you to know that. I wanted you to know what that son of a bitch did to me. I wanted you to know that when I finally got the nerve to tell my Mother *Zozed* that she stood by me. She told him to pack his things. And he left. And we never saw him again. And I am so forever grateful to her for believing me, for rescuing me from that.

My head lay resting on her lap by then, and I was crying, of course. And Nooko was stroking my hair like she would always do when I was upset. Comforting me. And I realize now, of course, that it should have been the other way around.

I suppose when I die and cross that river, that son of a bitch might be there waiting for me, as well. I suppose I've thought about what I might say to him, you know?

I carried all of this, I don't know, anger and resentment toward him for so many years, for such a long time. And finally I had to just let it go, to forgive myself.

Nooko. What do you mean forgive yourself? Forgive yourself for what? You were just a little girl. You were the victim.

I had to finally forgive myself. Forgive myself for all of those years of anger and resentment because I allowed what he did to me to fester in me for all of those years, and I carried all of that and in doing so, it controlled me. Do you understand, do you see? I had to let it all go. It was the only way I could move on. And when I did it was like this terrible burden was lifted from me.

And none of that is to say that every once in a while anger and resentment don't creep inside my thoughts whenever I think back to those terrible, terrible times.

Sometimes it's good just to give it a voice.

That son of a bitch.

Nooko went on to tell me that she not only had to forgive herself, but she also had to forgive him. Me, I didn't get that. I didn't think I could do that. Not ever. Not for anything like that. Me, I would have wanted to hunt him down and cut off his penis with a dull, rusty knife and shoved it down his throat until he choked on it. Me, I think there are some things that are not forgivable.

F--- that Tao forgiveness shit.

Somehow after she told me that we managed to move on to other things. Sometimes that is the only thing that can be done—move on. She told me about living in New York. I still can't believe she lived there. I never thought she left Bresette Hill (a neighborhood in Red Cliff village) her entire adult life.

I did. I left Bresette Hill for two years and went to New York. This is how it happened. Like I mentioned a bit earlier, I was good at sewing, and Mother *Zozed* taught me all she knew. By the time I was in high school, I was designing and making my own clothes. And I had some talent with art as well—pencil, charcoal, and watercolors. In high school, when there was a banner or poster that needed to be designed, I was the one the art teacher recruited to design and draw it. So in my senior year of school my home economics teacher pulled me aside and told me that there was a way to combine my ability to design and make clothing with my art. She had a sister who worked in the fashion industry in New York who would very much like to take on an apprentice, and wanted a local girl from her hometown. And I have to tell you, when she said that I was thrilled beyond belief.

When I told my mother about it that night, I wasn't sure what she was thinking straight away because she got really quiet. Then Mother *Zozed* came and sat by me, and I remember she took my hand and talked real soft, and I could tell she was real proud of me.

"My Genevieve," she said, "when you first came into this home many years ago, I was afraid. I think I feared that out of the blue someone from the agency would come knocking on the door and say they made a mistake, and that they were taking you away. And for years I feared that, and I think I would have died if it ever had happened. Your journey here so many years ago was filled with such heartache and I just didn't want to see you hurt anymore. I, for one, will have trouble letting you go. I know, however, that you need to go out into the world sometime."

So in late summer of 1938, in the heart of the Great Depression, with the blessings of my mother and a loan from my home economics teacher for fare, I boarded a train from Ashland bound for Milwaukee, then on to Chicago and then New York. And when I arrived at Penn Station in New York I was met by Miss Elsie Simms, my teacher's sister, who took me on a tour of the city via the subway and sidewalks, and then to her small apartment in Chelsea, where I was provided a cot in her sitting room and made to promise I would find part-time work to help pay the rent and contribute to groceries.

Although most of the leading designers of the day came out of Paris, New York was still a top fashion design mecca. Elsie Simms, my mentor, worked for McCall's, the leading pattern design company in its day, designing dresses for everyday people and everyday wear. As her apprentice, I got to work side by side with her throughout the entire design phase, from idea to sketches, to assisting at selecting pattern materials—cloth, closures, buttons, thread—we might suggest to the higher-ups. Everything the company did was designed and made in-house before it ever made it to the pattern stage and the catalog books. For my work I received a very small apprenticeship wage, nothing really to write home about, not even close enough to live on. But what an amazing opportunity it was! And, I was in New York.

I didn't have much in terms of spare time during the workweek, but during the few breaks I had, and the rare day off, I began the search to find out about my Irish family. There were things I needed to know, the empty spaces in my heart to fill, that really had nothing to do with my adoptive mother. I will always love her deeply, and I know she would have approved of what I was doing by looking for information on my birth parents, as well my brother.

Just the mere thought that maybe they were there still in the city, the constant wondering about my past, was like the missing pieces of a puzzle.

And it's quite a story, but eventually the Catholic Aid Society released what they knew about my family.

So that's what I know, and I guess it's enough for now. I'll tell you the rest but it better be soon, before I cross that river.

She pointed in the direction of the vast Ojibwe sky, the Path of Souls (Milky Way), and to the northern lights, who are the spirits of all of our ancestors dancing in the spirit world, in a place where there is only happiness.

Of course I didn't last forever in New York.

After I'd been there for nearly two years, I got a letter from one of my aunties that my mother had become very ill. There used to be a lot of flu and things like that back then, and we didn't have all the medicines you see nowadays. Anyway, she said I should come home, before it was too late.

So that's what I did. I gave up all of that, what I had, what I was doing out there and came home. And I never went back. My mother got better eventually, and she lived for many more years, and I'd like to think it was because I was there for her, nursing her.

But you gave up so much, Grandma Nooko. I mean, New York, the fashion industry. You gave all of that up and you came back here.

I did. It wasn't easy, I suppose. Even now sometimes I think about the what ifs. And my Mother *Zozed*, who I loved so dearly, I have to admit that I felt some resentment that I came back here. Maybe I would have stayed out there if she hadn't gotten ill. It was the opportunity of a lifetime, you know, one very few people are given. I felt guilty for even having ever thought that way. How could I have felt that toward someone who gave me so much, who sacrificed so much for me?

Yin and yang, shadow and light, it's always going on inside us. And which one wins?

Which do we allow to win?

In the end, though, by coming back I used the skills I acquired in New York to design all kinds of outfits, the beadwork with all its colors and designs, the moccasins.

And I was able to actually use all the other knowledge I'd acquired from my mother—the language, stories. I was active in the lodge (traditional ceremonies) until just a few years ago. If I had stayed in New York, I would never have been able to use any of that. Who in New York would I have been able to speak Ojibwe with? Who would want to know about making outfits? Who would wear my moccasins? Where would I have been able to attend ceremonies?

I suppose that somewhere way deep down inside I still sometimes wonder how my life may have been different if I had stayed there. It's natural to think that way. I suppose, even now after all these years, there is still some regret. It's natural to feel that way.

That is what life is.

In the end, though, I returned here. This land had become my home. I missed my people and this place too much.

AFTER THAT DAY I stopped more often to visit Grandma Nooko to hear her story. It is a beautiful story, sacred in every way. Even now when I share it I hold that asemaa, *tobacco, in my hand as I recall it.*

Grandma Nooko walked on almost a year ago. By then, of course, we had shared all of our secret stories. I have a whole collection of sons of bitches that she, even in death, is teaching me to forgive. And before she passed, she gave me her copy of the book Tao Te Ching *by Lao Tzu, given to her by her teacher.*

I've dog-eared that sucker like a mad woman.

The path gets lighter that way.

This past spring I made a journey east for her, for a great-grandmother known for making beautiful Ojibwe dance outfits and beadwork, for all of her dreams of what was and could have been, for the lands she left. In New York, I went to the mass burial site where nearly a million immigrants, the Irish and other poor, homeless, stillborn, or former prisoners lie buried on Hart Island, where I recited a prayer bequest of my great-grandmother in the language of her adopted people, the Ojibwe. And then I journeyed on further east to County Clare in Ireland, where I walked the roads and fields of Nooko's Irish ancestors, and where I again put that sacred asemaa *to* aki, *our mother earth, and recited the same prayer, which I now share with you:*

Gichi Manidoo
daga
wiidookawishin weweni
ji naanaagadawendamaan
ji

odaapinamaan
iniw
ge-gashkitoosiwaan
ji
aanjisidooyaan
ji
de-apiichide' eyaan
ji
aanjisidooyaan
ge-gashkitooyaan
ji
-de-apiichinibwaakaayaan
ji
gikendamaan
ono

God, grant me the serenity to accept the things I cannot change, courage to change the things I can, and wisdom to know the difference.

Sara's Song

I've been thinking of you a lot lately, Sara. In my dreams we are both children again, walking home from that Catholic mission school where we were reminded we were sinners and heathens who would surely go to hell if we didn't change our ways. You in a worn print dress your mother found in the back room of the church, in the boxes of free clothes. Me in my bib overalls and hook boots with broken and tied-together laces. That's how I remember things, Sara. You will always be perfect to me. I don't want to remember you drunk and smelling of other lovers. I don't want to remember you like that.

I don't even know why I'm talking to you. You've been gone for years now. But I know there are times when your memory comes to sit beside me.

My life is filled with everyday things that sometimes jolt my memory back to other times, other chapters in my story. At no particular place or time of day, a certain movement of clouds or wind will take me back to the times we would walk into your house, where your mother sat darning socks in the kitchen. In my memory there was a wind causing yellowed lace curtains to sway and dance to her songs. I remember you had her gift of music. And for just a moment when I'm thinking these things, there will be a longing. Or I will be walking down the street and suddenly become immersed by the smells of a certain perfume you would wear, and I will be reminded of your warm and gentle voice. I will smile slightly, and if I'm with someone they might ask me about my smile, and I will say it's nothing special. But it will be. There are other times when I will want to see you and touch you and be with you so much I will be overcome with longing. Maybe I will be out driving alone and a song on the radio will gently touch me on the shoulder. I may have to pull over to the side of the road, my hands will go to my face, and I will again grieve as if it were the first day of my grieving. At times like that it is as though your memory has come to sit beside me, to hold my hand, to remind me the past and present are one and the same.

This is one of those times.

BROTHERS AND SISTERS can sometimes intuitively sense when even small things are amiss with the other, and they find ways to provide support in difficult times in subtle and indirect ways. So when Eddie pulled his old pickup truck into the Andrews' yard, he sensed there was something wrong. There was a manner in his brother's movement about the yard, the way he would work for short bursts, then stop and look off in the distance. There was a look in his eyes that could not hide his disappointment about something, and a meandering tone in his voice. He had recognized these things about his brother for many years.

He remembered back to a particular winter when they were little boys, and they had gone snow sledding with their cousins. Their grandfather had made them a toboggan from a long piece of sheet metal, and it was recognized as the fastest sled on the rez. It was faster than the car hoods that other rez kids used as sleds, much faster than the slickest piece of cardboard. Their metal toboggan easily outdistanced the town kids' storebought ones. So a partic-ular day when they went sledding down the steepest hill in Red Cliff and made a direct hit on the only poplar tree in the way, they hit it faster and harder than anyone had ever hit it before. Five little rez kids went flying in all di-rections, their handmade wool mittens and charity winter boots filled with snow. Clods of snow collected on the knitted scarves their grandmothers had made for them, and snow jammed up their tattered and dirty army surplus winter coats. And when everything cleared and they began picking themselves up, Eddie noticed his brother remained motionless on the ground.

"We better get him home, " one of his cousins had said. So four little rez kids loaded their cousin and brother up on a toboggan, which now would forever wear a dent in commemoration of that day, and began pulling him home. Halfway up another hill on their way home, Eddie noticed a stir in his brother and motioned for the others to stop. The injured little boy slowly opened his eyes and reached out his hand to his older brother. There was a certain look in his eyes, one of fear and love and pain, and Eddie said to him, "Are you going to be all right?"

And the love he had for his little brother would show in other difficult life times. As the years passed and they found themselves grieving the passing of family members, their grandparents and mother and father and aunties and uncles, and cousins, Eddie would always find ways to seek out his brother, to visit him, and sit with him. At times like this he would enter his brother's house early in the morning to make him coffee and bring it over to him when he arose for the day. If his brother was working on his car or boat, he would pick up a tool and begin helping him with a repair. Always there would be talking between them just above a whisper, and light laughter, but for the most part there was little said. So many Indian people are that way. And they would glance into each other's eyes to acknowledge that one was there to be there for the other and the unspoken understanding would be, "Are you going to be all right?"

"Uh-huh."

So it was that day Eddie went to visit his brother. He moved in his quiet way, picking up his brother's net boxes and putting them in the shed. When the work was done, they sat on the porch, and Eddie pulled out a pocketknife and began whittling away at a stick of wood.

"Did you see Ronnie last night over on Madeline Island?"

"Uh-huh."

"He got in trouble over there."

"That's too bad."

Enough said.

It wasn't as if this was the first time Eddie had heard of his nephew's bad behavior. He remembered just the past winter when Ronnie had beat the hell out of some white kid for some stupid nothing reason. This was just after

Eddie had spoken to Ronnie's class, where he had been telling the students, especially Ronnie, how as people we need to live a certain way, a gentle way, and how we need to be respectful. These ways of living and being meant so much to Eddie that whenever he spoke to groups about these things, his voice would always crack with emotion.

"Listen to me," he would say. He would speak from the heart.

He remembered Ronnie sitting in that classroom, respectful and looking proud of his uncle, and occasionally nodding his head in acknowledgment and agreement. Then he remembered hearing that after the talk his nephew seemed to forget everything that had been said. And now his nephew had been drinking, just after hearing his uncle talk to him and the other young people about the importance of knowing their history, and about living a certain way. He remembered being so proud just last night when Ronnie had handed him some tobacco, feeling this was just another reminder that his nephew knew the importance of giving back, of thanking and acknowledging elders and people who know traditional ways.

And he was thinking, *why is it we are so weak? We try to be good, so many of us. But our shadow sometimes calls us to dark places. Always we need to work on living the gentle way.*

The fact his only nephew was misusing alcohol brought a special kind of foreboding to Eddie for too many reasons. Alcoholism had played center stage for too many years in his own life. He knew first hand how it could steal a person's soul and blind them to give up everything good and right. Eddie had buried too many uncles and cousins and friends who had driven through trees or been kicked to death in drunken brawls, or who had died in drunken stupors after swallowing their tongues or from throwing up and choking on their own vomit. He had seen too many elders lose their dignity when drunk, having peed in their pants or passed out in cars and yards and even on the sides of roads. He had seen how alcohol made people laugh too loudly and too easily. And Sara. All of Sara came flooding back to him that day.

He looked at his brother and stood up and walked into the house, and his hand lightly brushed him on the shoulder as he went by. Just for an instant their eyes met and their looks said, "Are you going to be all right?" A response, "Uh-huh." A slight smile.

EDWARD BAINBRIDGE had been in love with Sara Ann Bear a thousand years before they met as little children the first day of ricing (wild rice) season at a canoe landing, because there is a love that is sometimes born and passed down through generations, only to find its way to where it belongs. Their families had been ricing a small lake just south of Ashland, and every day early in the morning the parking area and boat landing would begin filling with old Model T Indian cars and pickup trucks full of parents and all of their children. The adults, for the most part, all knew each other. They were neighbors, some, or relatives, or had met at summer pow-wows or at other ricing lakes. They greeted and conversed with each other in familiar ways, ancient ways.

"*Aneen ezhi a yah yan* (Hello, how are you)?"
"*Nimino, aya.* (I'm fine)."

Quiet laughter. Old-time Indians always laughed that way. The thumping and clunking of canoes unloading, car doors closing, and older children being given instructions on caring for their siblings. Coughing, a smoker's cough. Late summer smells of mud and reeds and fish, and leaves just beginning to think fall.

"Now you watch your sisters and brothers. Don't let them go in the water. Make them stay at the landing. Make them share lunch," a mother would say, the last part with special emphasis toward the one child everyone has who doesn't know how to share.

"And no fighting, either," a mother would say, looking over at the younger children. "And you listen," she would say to a child who she knew would inevitably both fight and not listen before the day was out.

Eddie and his little brother would be cared for by their Auntie Marilyn, who was nine years old. She was a good babysitter because she let them do anything they wanted to do.

"I made you kids some potato sandwiches (sliced potatoes and pepper on homemade bread). And cake (chocolate, no frosting, just a large chunk wrapped in wax paper). And tea (a half gallon jug). And, Eddie, you leave your brother alone, too."

Eddie glanced to the side, plotting.

Then before anyone had a chance to think about being alone without adults for the day, their father and mother were off in the canoe along with the other ricers, with some twenty-odd children left on the banks of the lake for the day.

Always on the first day of ricing, the kids tended to stay near their cars until they became familiar with their surroundings. As soon as their parents left, many of them went back to the cars to get some more sleep. The more outgoing boys began bartering with each other over lunches, slingshot rubbers, marbles, agates, and other trade goods that lived in their pants pockets.

"I'll trade you this potato sandwich for one of your jam ones."

"I have cookies. Oatmeal (oatmeal cookies had a higher trading value than, say, sugar cookies). Trade for some of that?" Lips would purse and point to a piece of cake, a muffin, *lugalate* (a pan bread), fry bread, or some other treat. Even the young people pointed the old-time Ojibwe way, with their lips.

There was no trading for NBA basketball cards or video games. In those days, everyone was poor, but no one knew it because it was before the war on poverty. Hand-me-downs in the form of tattered jeans, yellowed t-shirts, faded print dresses, and shoes without laces were the fashions of the day. All the kids smelled like kerosene oil or wood smoke, or both. Slingshots and mud pies ruled.

Eddie and his little brother sat in the back seat of their father's car drinking tea and sucking on crackers while their auntie slept in the front seat. It wasn't until Eddie left for his second pee break of the day and was returning to the car, rounding the rear bumper of his father's old Chevy, that he saw for the first time the girl who would become the woman he would forever be in love with sitting in the back seat of her father's car, all hazel-eyed and faded blue flower-print dressed. All four years old of her. For when his small dark eyes met hers and he gave her a slight smile, and she gave him one of those, "You smell bad" looks, even though he was only six years old at the time, he knew.

They didn't say a word to each other that day, or in the days that followed, but Eddie would find ways to observe the little girl as she played with her friends. If she noticed him, and he would make sure of that in some way, he would give her his slight smile. Through days of playing cowboys and Indians, shooting slingshot rocks out into the lake, playing hide and go seek, trading marbles, and picking on his younger brother, Eddie would always find the time to go running past the little girl, or he would say something purposely loud enough for her to hear, just so she would notice him. Eventually one day she noticed he was noticing, and on the second-to-last day of ricing on that lake she returned his smile, this little girl who even at the age of four made good mud pies. On the last day he worked up the courage to say to her in a laughing way, "I'll trade you half of my potato sandwich for one of your mud pies."

To which she replied, "I don't like potato sandwiches."

But there were other lakes to rice and other boat landings in which the kids would play while their parents worked, and eventually Eddie and Sara Ann became friends.

Except for the times they saw each other at the ricing landings each year, the two rarely played together. When Sara was old enough for school, she rode the rez bus to St. Mary's Catholic School along with Eddie. She was, however, two years younger and, therefore, in a different peer group. Eddie was a Red Cliff village kid and Sara lived far out of town, and with the exception of school and ricing, she rarely ventured from home. So it wasn't until they were older, fourteen and sixteen respectively, that they began really noticing each other in hormonal ways.

It turned out that Sara lived out in Frog Bay, rural Red Cliff to some, if living in a remote community in northern Wisconsin could ever have places more isolated. She, along with nine brothers and sisters, lived in a small white frame house near the end of a long dirt tote road that wound its way out of Red Cliff and ended at the shores of Lake Superior some five miles out. Sara's mother was a quiet, dependent and enabling housewife, a white woman who could trace her French ancestry back to the sprawling vineyards near Bordeaux. Her father was a quiet, brooding alcoholic, whose binges would transform him into an abusive and neglectful man. He was one of those half-breeds, Sara told Eddie, who could pass for white and, therefore, was allowed in town bars still illegal for Indians to enter. He served as the drunken caretaker for several summer residents whose retreats far surpassed in size and splendor anything the rez residents could ever imagine themselves living in.

There was being poor, and there was being dirt poor, and Sara's family was the latter. Deer meat soup and pancakes were diet mainstays in her household, and Sara would tell Eddie when they were older how her younger and mildly retarded brother would often come running into the house after a wild day out playing in the woods. How he would dash into the kitchen and pull the cover off the kettle of what was on, proclaiming with genuine glee, "Oh boy! Pancakes!"

And that was after a month of pancakes.

She also told him of the times her father would use her as part of an excuse to go on one of his binges. How he would tell her mother that he needed to go into town to get his hair cut, and take Sara along as a decoy, thinking that if he took one of the kids along he would stay sober and actually do what he said he was going to do. But more often than not, Sara would end up sitting in her father's old car outside some bar for nights on end, where she would occasionally have to go inside to beg her father to take her home, or to get her a bottle of orange phosphate, a nut goody, or a pickled egg. Her first boy crush, she once told Eddie, was another young person sitting in a car next to her father's while his father sat drunk in the bar. She remembered once her father took her to a three-day party out near Makwah, where she played for days and late into evenings with strange children, all the while surrounded by adults who were always asking her name as they breathed their wine breath on her and laughed grotesquely until they passed out in chairs and on floors. And although she never would tell Eddie, she remembered another time when one of her father's drunken friends touched her in places that made her feel confused and dirty and shameful, making her sit on his lap while he bounced her up and down. When she was an adult and thought back to that incident, she would question how some of her own people could have moved so far away from their traditional ways that they would do these things to children. What hap-pened to them, she would ask herself. What has happened to us?

When these drunken binges ended, Sara would later tell Eddie, it was she who often had to drive home.

"I was just a little girl," she would say. "I was only seven or eight years old when I had to learn to drive. I couldn't hardly even see over the dash, and always my father would pass out, and there I would be driving home in the dark with those dim old car lights blinking through the trees."

When they made it home, Sara would say, she would sneak into the house and make her way to the bedroom, where she would find a place to cuddle in the warm sprawl of her sleeping brothers and sisters. She found comfort there, she would say. She knew the father who had taken her out on one of his binges, who had fed her pickled eggs and nut goodies from a bar, who had made her drive home, would become an enraged drunk before the night was out. Invariably, her father would awaken and start the car, only to find he was too drunk to drive. Sometimes he would roar up and down their long driveway, going forward and in reverse and in and out of the ditch. Once he hit the house, shaking everyone out of bed. At other times he would sit out in the car with the headlamps on, roaring the motor and honking the horn, as if to proclaim to the world he was home, the lord and king of the domain was home, wanting the attention afforded to those who ruled over domains. And always, she would say, there would be a special dread when he entered the house, so much so she remembered her stomach muscles cramping up she was in such fear of him, because the quiet man who was her father when he was sober would transform into an abusive ogre.

There he would sit at the kitchen table, tapping his foot on the floor and singing some song he heard at the bar.

"Get me something to eat," he would proclaim to a house that was filled with his frightened and silent children, as well a frightened wife.

"Why don't you just go to bed," their mother would say. But he would call her something demeaning.

"You're nothing but a fuckin' whore," he would yell. "Get your fat ass out here and get me something to eat."

So while his children lay frightened in bed, their mother, the woman who bore his children, would arise and enter the kitchen, carrying the household's only kerosene lamp with her. Sara would later tell Eddie how at times like this she was embarrassed for her mother, for the degradation she had to endure, and how she once could no longer bear to hear any more abuse and went into the kitchen to confront her drunken father.

"You leave her alone! You leave my mother alone!" she screamed.

"You get out of here, you little shit," he yelled, coming after her. She remembered running from the house, and seeing her father hitting her mother as she stepped in to intervene. She remembered her little brothers and sisters sobbing and sleepy and frightened, running out with her into the cold and dark of night. Of them running out to the dark cleave of the field and hiding behind trees, while their father stood at the door with his gun, proclaiming he was going to kill "all you little bastards." And she remembered her mother sitting in the tall, wet, late evening grass with the two smallest children, sobbing.

She told Eddie about how her father once sold their icebox while on a bender and how two town men came into their home one afternoon and sheepishly told her mother that they had bought it from her husband. Sara would never quite get over her mother putting what little was in the ice box onto the floor, and how, later, she would come upon her mother crying softly in a corner of the one bedroom they all shared, sitting in her old rocker, her fingers touching her lips, her eyes filled with disappointing tears from too many years of unfulfilled dreams and broken promises. She would never forget, she once told Eddie, how when her mother died her father so mourned her passing he seemed to forget all the awful things he had made her endure, this woman who had given up all her promise to a man who so selfishly took all her pride, all her dreams.

Unlike Sara's family, Eddie was raised in a functional home by parents who didn't abuse alcohol, and who believed that children were precious gifts given to them, entrusted to them. So while he found himself to be a good listener to Sara's stories and could empathize with her, his life had not taken him down that path.

How was it these childhood friends would become lovers? How was it that friends who sat next to each other on the school bus each day, or friends who shared a potato sandwich at summer catechism or during ricing season, or friends who passed and acknowledged each other during the long walking circles at summer pow-wows would one day notice each other in the ways of lovers? What was it about fate and luck and timing and circumstance that took people to certain places and put certain events before them that forever changed their life path? Eddie tried to pinpoint it down to a day, a moment.

Always at pow-wows there are eagles, and once when Eddie and Sara stood leaning against the rail that separated the dance area from the rest of the pow-wow grounds, she would say, "I'm from eagle clan. My dad's dad, my grandpa, was a white man. So I have to be."

Maybe then they both realized it was appropriate in the eyes of the community that they would begin to see each other as lovers, for to see each other in that way and to be from the same clan would have prompted a talk from one of Sara's Ojibwe aunties, or from one of Eddie's paternal uncles. Eddie knew his father was bear clan because the home he grew up in was filled with bear memorabilia, pictures of bears, a bear wall hanging, a bear claw necklace hanging from a family photograph. His father had told him they were part bear.

"What part of me?" Eddie remembered asking.

"Those beady little eyes," his father had said, laughing. But Eddie also had a way of extending his lower lip when he pointed to things, the ways bears do. *I think my lips are part bear, too,* he thought.

That is also where timing came in, because if they had been born just a generation earlier, neither their courtship nor eventual marriage would have been allowed. Sara's parents would have arranged for her marriage, and she may not have found out about who was to be her life partner until the day of her marriage. In those times there was no refusing, or questioning the decisions of parents. That was not the way. But times had changed. What was considered culture had changed.

Sara Ann Bear was seventeen years of age when she married Edward James Bainbridge in the tiny Catholic church in the village of Red Cliff, the same church where as babies they had been baptized, where they had attended their first and second communions under the stern tutelage of nuns who didn't want to be teaching reservation children, and where they had been officially confirmed by a now long dead bishop. Neither was a practicing Catholic. Sara lived too far from town to attend Mass. Eddie was Catholic by default. One of his grandmothers shamed his mother into it. In many ways his family still followed their traditional ways, and he attended ceremonies the church would certainly have banned if they knew of them.

Like so many rural village churches, this was both a place of great joy and great sadness, and even when the church pews were filled for such a joyous occasion as a wedding, there were the remembrances of times of loss and grieving. Among the people of Red Cliff that day there was a collective recognition that the circle of life is a dance of light and shadow, of extended times of sunlight and winters where nights will not end. Just a year earlier in the same church, Sara had attended the funeral of her sister. A carload of drunks sliding off an icy road. One of her brothers had rushed into the house to tell an already unhappy home of a horrible accident. Sara and her mother and brothers and sisters had rushed to the accident scene. There her younger sister lay trapped in a car that had careened into a power pole while on a drunken joy ride. But what would haunt her most was the memory of having to hold her mother back as the fire and rescue crew tried to free the girl from the car. Of her mother standing knee deep in snow in the dead of winter without boots or a coat, crying, "Oh, my God! My little baby!" Her mother would scream over and over again, long after the priest would come to them in the emergency room at Washburn hospital and tell the family a daughter and sister had died.

Even as she was walking down the aisle of the church, with her half-drunken father holding her arm, she thought of her sister, of the smatter of blood and broken glass and then of her sister lying in a coffin wrapped in the hand-sewn quilt their mother had so lovingly made.

She thought these things even as she looked Eddie in the eyes and told him she would love him forever, in sickness and in health, until death. Even when he whispered in her ear, "*Weedjeewaugun*" (my companion in the path of life). She felt great joy and great sadness at the same time. That was her path, her way.

After the wedding they took a long boat ride out into the blue of the lake and green of hills and islands in Eddie's family fish trawler. They were in love, and this woman who wore the burden of joy and sadness sang to her husband what would forever become their song, "*La vie en Rose.*"

Des yeux qui font baisser les miens
Un rire qui se perd sur sa bouche
Voilà le portrait sans retouche
De l'homme auquel j'appartiens
Quand il me prend dans ses bra
Il me parle tout bas
Je vois la vie en rose

(With eyes which make mine lower,
A smile which is lost on his lips,
That's the unembellished portrait
Of the man to whom I belong.
When he takes me in his arms
He speaks to me in a low voice,
I see life as if it were rose-tinted)

THEY MOVED INTO a small house Eddie had built with green lumber that stood in a clearing of clover and sumac up in the hills that overlooked Lake Superior. He worked long hours fishing commercially with his father. She was a housewife, and her days were filled with making quilts and canning and tending a garden and scrubbing floors down on her hands and knees. They dreamed of children. Her marriage to Eddie seemed to be an escape from her unhappy years of growing up. Although she missed her mother, as well the fields and woods of Frog Bay, she was quietly happy living with a man whose life didn't revolve around the episodes inherent to drinking binges. In the early years of their marriage, Eddie never drank anything stronger than coffee.

Sara desperately tried to give Eddie sons and daughters. She knew his fondness for children in the way he cared for her younger brothers and sisters, his cousins' children, and later in Eddie's younger brother's son, Ronnie. At first she just thought her inability to bear children was simply bad timing or bad luck. Later they would go to doctors in Washburn, and then to Duluth, where they would be told as they sat in a waiting room with Eddie holding her hand that they would never have a child. Her body had betrayed her. And she looked long in desperation into her husband's eyes, pleading for his forgiveness. He in his gentle way, his kind eyes and soft voice, his thin breath in her ear. His tears.

"*K'zaugin.*" I love you.

Sometimes there is a shame that cannot be swept aside and forgotten, that cannot be neatly folded and put away in cedar chests, cannot be given away in the confessionals at church. Sara would wear her shame through the remaining days of her life, its damp and cold embrace cloaked around her like a dark shawl. A vision unfulfilled.

So as the years passed and she sat alone in that small house while her husband worked out on the lake, she found herself moving into darker corners. At first just a drink of whiskey to take away the pain and allow her to face the day. And soon Eddie would come home to her wild-horse eyes.

"You've been drinking again," he would say quietly, as he made his own dinner and cleaned up the messes she had long given up on. "Why are you doing this?" His voice would trail off. He would say nothing else to her.

"Chrissakes, I only had one," she would say. She would look right through him when she said that, angry and defiant, still vulnerable.

What would be one day a month would become one day a week would become every day. Sometimes her drinking would keep Eddie away long into the evening. He didn't want to see his wife that way. And sometimes when he could no longer keep working on his boat or visiting relatives or working outside, he would come home to drink with her, and for a time his loneliness and anger and pain would leave him, too.

He remembered one time he came home and found her sober. They sat and reminisced of happier days and life events and things that would never be. He could not stop looking at her that day. Touching her, he was so overwhelmed with the love he felt. Just for a moment it seemed life returned to her eyes. Just for a moment that little girl he had met long ago at a wild rice boat landing was there in that room with him. But the next day when he came home she was drunk and sitting in a chair listening to the radio, and when he said something to her she called him a son of a bitch and slapped him, and slapped him again and again until he walked outside to get away and sat on the steps while she locked the door and drank until she passed out and he had to bust in the door of his own house so he could sleep with his drunken and unconscious wife.

And one Thanksgiving she spent sitting drunk in a dark corner of their house and Eddie went to his younger brother's for dinner, where an especially nosey cousin asked why he was there without Sara.

"She's not feeling well." He lied. But there was that look in his eyes, and a recognition of his brother's part, a look long recognized by the two brothers.

There were other times he would return home from the lake to find her gone, and on those times he would sit long into the night awaiting her return from the bars. Eventually, a car would sneak its way down the driveway at some odd hour of the night, and she would emerge drunk and laughing. He would climb into their bed and pretend he was asleep, but sleep would rarely come on nights like that. And there would be other times she would not return until the next day, or the day after. He would be unable to go to work and become frantic, thinking what fate might have come of her. Waiting for a sheriff's car to pull into his drive and tell him they had found his wife dead in a ditch somewhere, or twisted around a light pole, or beaten to death outside a bar. But mostly he would wonder with whom she was sleeping, who her lovers were.

Even though most adults in Red Cliff knew of Sara, they remained for the most part nonjudgmental of her. That was the way of so many Indian people, an acknowledgment that each carried their own unique burden, their own pain. Eddie was well respected in the community. He had a way about him, an ancient way, a gentle way. There was depth in his words. People listened to him and respected him.

Because of the esteem in which he was held, he was often asked to speak to groups. There was a particular time he spoke at an honor luncheon for the high school graduates from the village of Red Cliff. He remembered telling them about living their lives in a certain way, of the importance of giving back, of being humble and respectful, and about not allowing themselves to be controlled by anger, or by alcohol. But when he returned home from his speech, he found his wife passed out drunk in a lawn chair in the yard. He walked past her into the house and sat on the couch and put his hands to his face and wept for all the anger and humiliation and despair of his life.

"Why are you doing this to me?" he pleaded with his Creator. "Why are you doing this to me?"

But for all of the challenges the Creator had put before him, none was to be a greater burden than the time of an early winter morning visit from his younger brother, whose hesitant tapping on the door would shake him from a ragged dream with a start, and he would open the door to find his brother standing before him. That look in his eyes, a recognition. That day his brother had to tell him of the police finding Sara frozen to death in the back seat of someone's car. And just for an instant, upon hearing the words of that forever-horrible moment, a flood of memory rushed before him. Of a little hazel-eyed girl in a faded blue flower-print dress.

Although Sara was given a Catholic burial service, Eddie grieved for her in the old way. He offered food to her spirit and built a mourning fire near the cleave of woods by the cemetery, which he tended for four days until Sara's spirit reached the land of souls. He would no longer live in the house he had built for them because everywhere were the reminders of Sara. Some people so define a place that without them these places lose their spirit, their meaning. And one night in the depths of his grief he poured gasoline on what was their home and burned it. He drank hard and laughed too loud and too easily.

The pain was so bad his laughter could be heard for miles.

SEVERAL DAYS AFTER RONNIE had been expelled from summer school on Madeline Island, Eddie came into his brother's house and found the boy sitting in front of the tel-evision set, glued to it. Hypnotized by it so much his hand would sometimes altogether miss the bag of Cheetos he was feasting on. His brother and sister-in-law were sitting at the kitchen table, drinking coffee and separating grocery coupons. Teasing each other. Eddie went to the counter and helped himself to a cup of coffee. He poured in too much sugar and cream and stirred it with a butter knife. They talked, all of th em realizing h ow precious these talks were in the course of their lives. And among the adults, there was recognition that Eddie had a purpose for being there that day. There were reasons for each word, each inflection of voice, each gesture. His stories had deeper meaning. He began.

"You remember when I was a drunk?" he said to his younger brother. "I was drunk for a couple of years and didn't work and didn't bathe and didn't give a shit and—"

"Chrissakes, for a while you lived in that old shed out there." His brother pointed with his lips outside the door to a sagging shed slowly sinking into the swamp that surrounded their yard. They laughed.

Ronnie sat in the other room, his eyes glued to the television set. Munching on Cheetos.

"I've been sober now for ten years." Eddie showed the adults his sobriety pin.

"Thanks to me." His brother.

"Me, too." His sister-in-law. They all laughed again.

They told all the drunk stories that day. This went on for a long time. Their conversations were a litany of car accidents and long-dead cousins, bar fights, ugly girlfriends, near misses from beer bottles and knives and bullets, glancing blows and fate and timing and luck and circumstance. Just loud enough to echo into the living room. Just loud enough for Ronnie to hear. They talked this way until Ronnie's parents stood up and excused themselves.

"We need to go grocery shopping." They were lying.

When they left, Eddie went into the living room and sat on the couch opposite his nephew.

"How you doing, Nephew?"

"Uhhhhmm." Chewing. Staring at the television set. MTV.

"Did you hear us telling our drunk stories? I'm glad I don't do that anymore."

No response.

"I heard about what happened over at Madeline."

Ronnie's eyes looked down to the floor. He set down his Cheetos and turned down the television set. He listened to his uncle.

"Look at me." An uncle. His voice was shaking with emotion.

And that day an uncle told his nephew about how we should live our lives, and give honor to it by the way we live. About honoring others and being kind, and humble. The gentle way.

"There is a path we need to all try to follow. It is hard, I know. I have been there. I've failed many times. I know. My uncles used to tell me this. There is a certain way to live."

The story went on for the longest time.

And then it was over.

"What kind of music are you listening to?" An uncle.

"Hip hop. You like it?"

"It's okay, I guess. You ever hear what we used to listen to when we were young?"

"No."

"I'll go get some." Eddie got up and went outside to his old truck, returning with a cassette tape.

"How do you work this thing?" Eddie with his butt way up in the air on his hands and knees as he tried to load the tape into the tape deck and adjust the controls.

"This is something I can teach you, Uncle." A boy laughing.

The music began.

"*La vie en Rose.*"

An uncle and his nephew sat in the living room of an old house built with rough lumber, rummage sale windows, and mismatched furniture. The music consumed them and flowed out into the late summer air and around the odd collection of yard junk and blue of sky and smells of late summer, and a flood of memory came to an old man. Of a little girl he had met so many years ago, all hazel-eyed and faded blue flower-print dressed. All four years old of her. For just that moment she came and sat beside him and held his hand.

"*K'zaugin.*" I love you. A tear.

He didn't even realize he had said it aloud.

His nephew gave him that look, a recognition, and they said to each other in a way that had been passed down for many thousands of years among the People, in silence.

"Are you going to be all right?"

"Uh-huh."

Gekinoo'amaagejig (The Ones Who Teach)

Once there was a dancer with Down syndrome in full regalia at my reservation's sobriety pow-wow. At one point the announcer began reading the names of those on the sobriety list, and the length of their sobriety. And they all lined up, those sober for a day and those who had been sober for decades. It didn't matter. They lined up in the circle of the dance area and he was among them. He was so happy out there, so filled with joy, shaking hands and giving hugs. And when I saw him there, I looked all around to the other dancers and to the crowd sitting in the bleachers. And I was thinking, that is how we should be. We should be filled with the same pure joy. We should put the night behind us and begin a new day.

~Thomas D. Peacock

When I go for my walk, Davie's dog, Niibish, comes with me. He likes to run, though, and sometimes he chases cars and then I have to yell at him.

"No, Niibs. Those cars are going to get mad at you." But he don't listen good. I run out and try to chase him with a stick but I get too tired sometimes.

I sawed 'Livia, my Gramma Nooko's friend, on my walk today. She yelled out her window to me.

56

"Hey, Deacon, is that dog taking you for a walk again?"

"Niib's my bestest dog buddy," I yelled back to her. And I smiled so big it almost took up my whole face. That 'Livia and Gramma were bestest buddies, too, and when they went for walks, I got to go along. Now that Gramma's gone, all 'Livia does is sit there in her chair and look out the window.

I miss my Gramma Nooko. Grampa, too. I hug their pictures when I go to bed at night and I talk to them and I sing "Chocolate Ice Cream Cone" all to myself. Gramma used to sing that song to me every night when she put me down to bed.

September 8, 2015
TO: Delores Butterfield, Director
    Pine Bend Tribal Housing Division

FROM: Philip Larson, M.S.W.
    Family Social Worker
    Tribal Social Services
RE: Deacon Kingfisher

As you know, the tribal council granted Social Service's formal request to allow Deacon to remain in elderly housing despite the fact he does not meet the age criteria set by the Office of Housing and Urban Development (HUD) and reinforced by tribal ordinance. While we concur with you that the decision may cause your office some problems with the regional HUD office, we realize it was the best decision so far as Deacon is concerned. I'm just sorry we had to go to the council to override the decision of the tribal housing board.

Deacon is certainly capable of living independently, despite his cognitive limitations. To assist him we have assigned a home health aide to pay him visits twice a week to ensure he is maintaining his living unit, as well to make assurance he is getting proper nutrition and attending to his personal hygiene. ENP (Elderly Nutrition Program) will allow him to have lunch at the elderly center just as they would the elders of the reservation. He will be attending independent living training through the Bayfield County Developmental Achievement Center.

Deacon is making a difficult transition since the death of his grandparents, who until their deaths cared for him all thirty-six years of his life. We realize there may be issues from time to time because of this. We will work with your office in any way we can to ensure Deacon's residency in elderly housing is a smooth one for all concerned.

WE'VE BEEN AT A LOSS here at Pine Bend School ever since the elder Kingfishers were killed at Roy's Point in an accident with a drunk driver. That idiot drove straight through the stop sign like a bat out of hell and plowed into them sideways. He was a white guy who was shacking up with some Sisseton woman who moved onto our rez a year or so ago and got one of the low-rent units. That asshole lived, of course, but we lost those two precious elders. At least they went quick, the EMTs said.

You see, Joe and Shanud Kingfisher were our Ojibwe culture and language elder teachers. They came in twice a week and taught the language to our elementary and high school kids. And now, without them, we don't have anybody to properly teach it and just the thought of it makes me so afraid for our people. Because without the language passing down to the young generation, who is going to say those prayers to our Creator at our gatherings and ceremonies? The prayers can only be done in the language. Who is going to do the pipe ceremonies? That can only be done in the language as well. And who is going to do namings, and teach the young people about the healing plants, or the prayers and songs that go along with the practicing of skills like parching wild rice and making bark baskets and trapping? Joe did namings. He was the only one on our rez who had that gift. Shanud made the most beautiful black ash baskets. Very few people practice that craft anymore. I suppose skills like ricing and making maple syrup and stuff like that will survive in spite of the language, but wouldn't it be so much richer to know these things within the context of our Ojibwe language? To know the songs and prayers that should be said for the rice, or for the harvest of maple syrup? Without those two elder teachers, our community, our whole future as Native people, is in jeopardy. They were the last two people in our community, as far as I know, who were fluent Ojibwe speakers. At least as far as I am concerned, without our language we are just brown white people.

It isn't that any of us from the community hasn't tried to learn the traditional knowledge so we can pass it down to the young. Several of us in the thirty- to forty-year-old range have taken university courses in *Anishinaabe* (Ojibwe) history, culture, and language. My cousin Doris, in fact, is teaching Ojibwe history at one of the neighboring tribal community colleges. My friend Jerry, who I graduated from high school with, just got a new job at Lake Superior State teaching Native art classes. Me, I went all out like I've always done. Majored in American Indian studies from the U of Minnesota. Took three years of *Anishinaabe* language. I go to ceremonies on some of the other reservations to be around traditional people and to hear the language spoken and sung. When I have the time I drive the fifty or so miles down the road to Ogema, the next rez over, and sit in on their Thursday evening language table. Why? Because I know I will be an elder some day and young people will come to me for that knowledge. And when they do, I'd better know what I'm doing and what I'm talking about.

So I practice my Ojibwe every night while my wife is reading her mysteries, trying to nail down the language's complex verb structure, and all its inherent rules. It's such a complex language, more complex, at least that's what I've heard, than English. I wish I would have learned it as a kid, but neither of my parents spoke it. They had it beat out of them in boarding school. I told my wife I'm able to count to a thousand now in Ojibwe. She laughed when I said that, looking up over her book. But then that just got me thinking, what good is that? I need to know so much more than counting.

When the elder Kingfishers were alive, they mentored me in the language. Joe especially. Sometimes before and after their classes he would just speak the language to me, no English, and I would have to try to figure out what he was saying, or I would be shit out of luck. I would try to respond the best I could in the language, and I know that my pronunciation and enunciation weren't always right, but he never shamed me for not knowing the right way. He would never have done that. I remember once I was so frustrated with myself because I studied for so long and hard and I still just wasn't getting what he was saying to me. And I finally said to him, in English, "Joe, I'm so sorry, I can't understand what you are saying. I feel so damn bad about it. I want to know the language, you know."

I just stood there with my head down. I felt just bad then. But he was so patient with me, and he understood.

"This is not your fault, David. You have nothing to be ashamed of. You shouldn't blame yourself because you weren't brought up around the language. If there is anybody to blame it's that BIA (Bureau of Indian Affairs), when they outlawed the speaking of the language and forbid us practicing our ceremonies. So don't blame yourself. Give yourself credit for trying, for working to become a speaker. Most of all, give yourself time. Someday, and I think that day isn't too far off, you're going to answer me when I speak to you, and it'll be in our language. And when that day comes, David, oh, your gramma and grampa and all those old people who have walked on, they are going to be smiling. Oh, they will be smiling. They will be so proud."

So that day two months ago when I was sitting in my office at Pine Bend School and the phone rang and it was my mom, and she said that she heard on the scanner there was a bad accident at Roy's Point and that it was the elder Kingfishers, I just froze, because things like that aren't suppose to happen to such beautiful people like them.

"Mom," I said, and she must have been able to tell by the tone of my voice just how devastated I was. "Mom . . . no . . ."

She must have called my wife, because Liz was down in my office about five minutes later.

After the accident, I took the elder Kingfishers' places in the classroom as the children's teacher. I feel so inadequate there because I know just a small fraction of what those two elders knew. And the young ones know, they do, how important that language is because they remind me all the time. The other day one of the little ones came up to me after class, and he asked me something.

"David," he said (they call me David), "could you give me my Ojibwe name?"

"I would be honored to do that if I could," I said, "but I don't have that gift. Maybe when I get older I will. But right now, I can't do that."

The little boy walked away from me so disappointed, and the look on his face just said it all as far as I am concerned.

Now it's like a race, you know, to learn the language.

I been learning Niibish to speak and now he knows, too.
"Umbe, *Niibish!" (Come, Niibish!)*
"*Niibish,* namadabi." *(Niibish, sit.)*
My Grampa Nimishoo and Gramma Nooko always talked it to me. When I see them in my head they talk it to me.

I LIVE NEXT TO ELDERLY HOUSING, which sits just off a ways from the main rez housing project. I grew up right around there, in that same area. We lived in an old rez house in the middle of a field that was turned into a sprawling HUD neighborhood once the tribe had a building boom about twenty or so years ago. Now my old haunts are filled with fifty or more pastel green, blue, and yellow HUD houses, all looking alike. I remember when I was little I would go and hide in the deep grass of the field that was there, and I would pick daisies and buttercups and bring them to my mother. We were all poor then, all us Indi'ns. But we all got along and there was no fighting or crime or the alienation we see now. Now, it seems even our neighbors are strangers. Now in that field where I used to run there are houses, a couple of messy garbage racks, about a hundred rez dogs of all sizes, pedigrees, and colors, and a couple of old war ponies (cars) in every drive.

Sometimes I wonder if we didn't lose something in the process of modernization, something more important than indoor plumbing and forced-air furnaces and refrigerators.

Anyway, lately I've been seeing a lot of Deacon Kingfisher, walking up and down the road. Since his grandparents walked on he's been spending a lot of time with my dog, Niibish. I named Niibish for the Ojibwe word for tea, *anibishaboo*. See, when he was a little fellow, I picked him out at the pound and took him home for the first time, and I dunked him in a tub of sudsy water and scrubbed him up. The water was so dirty it was almost like I had dipped a tea bag in it. Just in case you wondered about that name. Us rez folks get our nicknames that way, too. There's a story behind every one of them—No Neck, Catfish Lips, Auk, Johnny Slippery. Every one of us, including our dogs, has a rez name. We have dogs named Cat, and cats named Dog, and dogs named Soup, and some are named after that crabby auntie everyone seems to have.

But Deacon has always been known simply as Deac. We're about the same age, so I really got to know him when we were little kids. Like I said, he was raised by his grandparents. I don't know what happened to his mom. When we were old enough for school we all rode that old orange bus to Pine Bend, where we had to endure twelve years of being told we were worthless by those teachers. I'd see Deacon on the bus every day with the rest of us, and out on the playground before and after school sometimes. But in school, he would disappear into the special classroom with five or six other kids with disabilities, and we'd never see each other all day. The bell would ring and their door would remain closed. They must have eaten lunch at a different time as well because we never saw them in the lunchroom. And of course, we never saw them at recess.

Every once in a while, of course, some jerk would pick on him and call him a retard.

"I'm no retard," he'd say. He would try to fight back with words, but the instigator would just mock him for it, and it seemed that fighting back would only make it worse.

For most of elementary school I put up with what the teasers were doing to him. Then in eighth grade or so, I just couldn't stand it anymore. Maybe by then I'd grown physically strong enough to have some confidence. That day there was some kid teasing Deacon on the school bus as usual.

"Leave him alone, eh?" I told the kid.

But the guy wouldn't quit. He wasn't even listening to me.

So I spoke a little louder and more in his face, like, "Leave him alone, I said."

He wouldn't quit, of course, so after we got off the bus I peppered his face with my fists and sent him home with his nose packed tight with toilet paper.

I was Deacon's hero after that.

Of course, not everything I did was worthy of a medal.

When I was a young warrior, my buddies and I used to have a lot of fun with Deacon. One time when we were about sixteen years old or so, we were driving around drinking beer and saw Deacon playing out in his grand-parents' yard so we decided to stop.

"Hey, Deacon," I remember yelling out to him. "Wanna come out with us and drink some beers?"

We were all laughing and shiny then, just getting a buzz on ourselves. And I suppose we were a bit bored and looking for some entertainment.

You see, back then we all had Deacon typed as the village idiot.

"Oh, no," Deacon said to me. "Gramma and Grampa would be *real* mad at me."

"Oh, come on," we egged him on.

I don't remember exactly what transpired to get him to come along but before you know it he was sitting in the back seat, packed between our girlfriends Judy, Luella, and Charlene, and off we roared out into the boonies to party.

It only took a couple of beers before Deacon was shit-faced drunk. By that time we boys in the front seat were trying to talk Judy into letting Deacon get some from her. She screwed just about anything that moved, and we fig-ured she wouldn't mind giving some to Deacon.

She wasn't drunk enough the first time we asked her, but as the evening wore on, she took us up on the offer and went off in the bushes with Deacon. I don't know if they ever did anything or not. Later on, I asked Deacon, of course.

"Hey, Deac, did you get any from Judy?"

"Secret," is all he said. He had a big smile on his face, and I still have no idea what did or didn't happen.

We dropped Deacon off in his yard just before sunrise. I often wonder what his grandparents thought when he came stumbling in their front door. And I wonder what they would have thought of me if they'd known it was me who took and got him loaded that night so many years ago.

Now, of course, I wouldn't even think of doing anything like that. Myself, I quit drinking years ago. My wife, Liz, has been sober for twenty years, and has a sobriety pin to prove it. And now I know more about my traditional beliefs, that our ancestors regarded people like Deacon as sacred beings, just as all of us humans are sacred in the eyes of the Creator.

Just because Deacon has Down syndrome doesn't mean he doesn't have a soul spirit. The Creator listens to him just as he does all of us, and the Creator watches over him as well, maybe even more than he would the rest of us. And Deacon has the same gifts from the Creator, the Creator's very essence, those values we were all born with.

I know that now.

So now when I see him with Niibish, I always make a point of stopping and talking with him.

"Hey, Deac," I say. I still call him that.

"Hey, Davey," he always says back.

I ask him how things are going and he'd talk forever if I let him. On and on he goes about what Niibish and him are up to, and about 'Livia, his grandmother's friend. Lately, he's been finding agates alongside the road. He gave me one of his favorites, giving it a big lick just before he handed it over to me.

I think what our tribal council is doing in allowing Deacon to live in elder housing is commendable. He needs to be cared for, like our elders. Like them, he has special needs. The fact the council is assuring he is eating regularly, and has assigned people to check on him every week, speaks well for all of us in the community. Deacon represents something to us, maybe standing as a symbol of how we Ojibwe should treat each other and care for each other.

I GOED OVER to 'Livia's lots, me and Niibish, so we can watch her TV. I told her I been learning Niibish the language. And she says she's knowed it since before she was born but now with Gramma Nooko gone there hasn't been no one to talk it to. So I started talking and pretty soon now she's talking with me that way. She says it's coming back inside her.

I WENT TO A CEREMONY last fall over near Crandon, and we were all sitting there in the teaching lodge. The speaker was talking in the language, of course, and he had a young man from Canada doing interpreting for him. Anyway, through the interpreter, the speaker told those of us who couldn't speak Ojibwe that we were born with all of that knowledge already inside us—the language, and those values for following that path, *mino-bimaadiziwin* (the Good Path). We just need to bring it out, he said. We need to want it real bad, and we need to go deep inside where it is and find it and bring it out.

Ever since I heard that I've been praying a lot. And one night I had this dream, in Ojibwe. In the dream I was speaking the tongue, and I could understand what the others were saying, and they understood me. When I awoke in the morning, I didn't want to get out of bed. I wanted to stay there in the dream. I didn't want it to end.

I don't know, but maybe something is happening now that is going to make that dream come true, and it's coming from someone I would have never dreamed of. See, one night my wife sent me to the store to get some change for the kids' school lunch tickets, and I saw Deacon and my dog out walking down the road. So I pulled over alongside them and rolled down the window. Anyway, Deacon was really concentrating on talking to Niibish about something and maybe he didn't see or hear me pull up by him. So I got to listen to him speak.

He was speaking in the language.

It was almost surreal. I was so stunned I pulled away and honked the horn and just waved at him, and he smiled and waved back to me.

It took me a while to settle down, but eventually I did. Later that evening I went over to elderly housing to visit him. I brought that sacred *asema* with me. He was in a pair of Tigger pajamas when he answered his door.

"Aniin ezhi a ya yan?" I said. How are you doing?

"Nimino aya, geendush?" He replied. I'm fine, and you?

"Nimino aya," I said back to him. I'm fine as well.

"Nimiwendum wabaminan," he replied. I'm happy to see you.

"Gidojibwem, ina?" he asked. Do you speak Ojibwe?

"Eya, baangi nindojibwem." Yes, a little Ojibwe I speak.

I asked him that night if he would be my teacher. And when he said he would, I gave him that sacred *asema*, tobacco, and he accepted it.

I've known Deacon nearly my entire life and for most of it I just thought he was a gentle and happy-go-lucky person who happened to have special needs. I never thought he would possess the knowledge and ability I have spent much of my adult life trying to get. Until now, I'd always measured him by his limitations.

September 30, 2015
TO: Pine Bend Local Indian Parent Committee

FROM: David Turner, M.Ed.
     Director of Indian Education
RE: Ojibwe language program

Your permission is requested to retain the services of Deacon Kingfisher as Ojibwe language teacher aide for ten (10) hours a week, $8.00 per hour beginning immediately through the reminder of the school term.

Deacon will work with me in the elementary and secondary Ojibwe language classes. He will be an excellent resource in the classroom given his fluency.

I WENT TO THE INDIAN parent committee meeting last night figuring my request to put Deacon on as a classroom aide would sail right through, no problem. So when my cousin Carolyn, chair of the committee, started raising all kinds of questions about whether Deacon should be working with the children, it really hit me sideways because I just had no idea she harbored that kind of ignorance.

I still can hear her whiney little voice now.

"Now, David, I just wonder if Deacon won't frighten the little ones. I mean, if you didn't know him that well, he could be kind of scary, don't you think? And don't we have to worry about the possibility of him doing something inappropriate? Do you remember when we were in catechism and Deacon was always doing the most inappropriate things—burping and *boogeting* (Ojibwe/English slang for farting). And as he got older he still did things like that every so often. And to be frank with you, I worry about his behavior around the little girls. Just because he's challenged doesn't mean he doesn't have urges. We would regret it for the rest of our lives if we allowed him to work with our children and something should happen."

My cousin Carolyn was never the brightest bulb on the tree. She did manage, however, to convince a majority of the parent committee to table my request. I tell you, I was so pissed I wanted to quit then and there. I have not been so angry in a long, long time. And it didn't matter what I said to counter her arguments. It was fifteen years ago when Deacon was doing those things in summer catechism, I said. He doesn't do that anymore. Everyone who works in the school, or drives a bus, has to have a background check. Deacon doesn't have a police record. He's never been in trouble with the law. He's never been accused of inappropriate sexual behavior directed toward children, or anyone for that matter.

"But David, don't you remember when we in the first grade, and a teacher was trying to teach Deacon how to use the drinking fountain and he got water all over himself? He was lapping at the water and laughing, and telling the teacher that he was a dog. Do you remember what he did? He took off every stitch of his wet clothes and put them in a big pile right there in the hallway next to the fountain. Now, is that the kind of person you want teaching our children?"

I had forgotten that Carolyn was one of the people on the tribal housing board who had voted against Deacon living independently in elderly housing. They said he should be in a group home setting. At least, that was their excuse. I think the other housing board members voted along with her simply because they felt they would get in trouble with HUD, who could come down on the rez for violating the federal age guidelines on who gets to live in elderly units. Apparently, you've got to be sixty-two years old to be considered an elder by HUD. I remember the day after the housing board had met and voted against Deacon, I went to visit Phil Larson, one of my old school buddies from the U, and he told me what happened. Phil is a white guy who married one of my other cousins, but he still has his head screwed on sort of right. We sat in his office and got just militant. What kind of Indians are going to let HUD, a federal agency, tell a tribe what to do?

We're a sovereign nation, aren't we? When are we going to start behaving like one? If we want one of our tribal members to live in an elderly unit, we should be able to do it. We should be telling them (HUD) what to do. My buddy Phil is acting like a member of the tribe now, aaayyy.

So anyway, after we sat in Phil's office and declared Pine Bend a sovereign nation, we marched on over to see our district rep. on the tribal council, and got her all fired up. That afternoon she led the charge at the council meeting and put that housing board in their place.

When we was watching Angry Birds I tolt 'Livia and Niibs that Davey says they said I can't be a teacher to the little ones. But that I can still be his teacher.

I spent the next couple of weeks lobbying the other parent committee members, behind Carolyn's back, to change their minds about Deacon. And I thought I got a majority convinced to give him a go. Well, it turns out I didn't even need to do that.

See, at the meeting the other night we were going through our regular business. Like, should we send a member to the National Indian Education Conference in Greensboro, North Carolina, or should we spend the $2,000 that would cost to buy hats and mittens for the kids? I mean, as far as I'm concerned we shouldn't even discuss that. Of course we should buy hats and mittens.

But that's the parent committee. Anyway, Carolyn had put my request to reconsider hiring Deacon as the last agenda item, and it was getting close to the time we would be discussing that.

So, about that time in the door comes, of all persons, 'Livia, a respected elder in our community, and Carolyn's auntie. You should have seen everyone's heads spin around when she came through that door. I was as surprised as they were because I had no idea she was coming there that evening. She sat quietly in the corner, not uttering a peep. Then when Carolyn said, "The last item on our agenda tonight is to reconsider the hiring of Deacon Kingfisher as Ojibwe language teacher aide."

'Livia stood then.

"I'd like to address the committee," she said.

Then she spoke to us in the language.

And her voice was at once so strong and forceful and gentle and sincere, and her message carried in it all the dreams of our ancestors who had walked on through the ages. She talked for a long time and then she sat down.

Then I told them what she said.

ME AND 'LIVIA AND DAVEY'S *teachers, Niibish. We teach that tongue to the little ones.*

Soft Wind

This little man came to my doorstep some time back. He obviously had walked to my place, or maybe somebody dropped him off down the road because I didn't see a car anywhere in sight. He seemed real nervous and talkative, and he looked Native in a messed-up sort of way. I was adopted out to a white family way back, he says, and now I want to find out my Indian ways like eagle feathers and trees having spirits and brotherhood with all creation. I want to make my own Indian costume, too, so I'll fit in, 'cause I want to move here to be with my Native brothers and sisters. Oh, I'm sorry, my name is Scottie, he said.

Who sent you to me, I asked, and he told me someone from the tribal center, and I asked who and he said some fat lady and that didn't help because there must be a hundred of them working there. So I just smiled because it seemed all the fat women in the village appeared in my mind all at once and they were all telling this little stranger to come see Eddie, that's me, and then, as he walked away from them, I could see them giggling like the joke's on me.

Like I say, he was Native, you could see that just by looking at him. And judging by the way he started jabbering away at me right away, maybe he was a little different.

So I panned him up and down with my beady little eyes. Then I let him in and told him to have a seat, and he found a tiny corner of the couch in the living room where he took up as little space as possible and sat there with his hands folded in his lap and looking around at everything on the walls.

You want some coffee, I asked, and he said no thanks, I just drink Coke, so I dug way back in the fridge and found a half-empty bottle of flat soda that had lost its fizz because some nephew forgot to put the cap on tight and I put it in a coffee cup and brought it in to him. I topped off my coffee while I was at it and returned to the living room and we just sat and stared at each other for a few nervous moments. And during that silence, I was wondering why it was people always sent me these lost souls and every new age white person type who wants an Indian name or had a dream they want deciphered.

So you want to learn how to dance like a real Indi'n? I asked. I was just teasing, but he didn't figure it out. He smiled back at me and asked if it was okay if he smoked. Before I could say a peep he had one in his mouth and was digging for matches.

I already know how to *sing* Indian, he said, and he started with one of those hi how are you's and tapping his feet with his eyes closed and while his eyes were closed, I took a closer look at him and wondered if I should have let him in. He was a wiry little guy for sure. Harmless, a child's mind, I concluded.

So when he finished singing for me, I asked where he'd been all these years and he told me his story. That went on for a couple of hours over the bologna sandwiches and

Kool-Aid I made up for lunch for the both of us. Turns out he had been raised by a white family somewhere down by Milwaukee, that he was twenty-seven years old. I know I'm from Red Cliff, this place, he told me at least five times. My ma, well my adoptive ma anyway, she told me that, he said. Anyway, he said, I been living with them until last year but then I met my wife, well, she wasn't my wife then, and we got married and we have a baby but she stayed back in Milwaukee because she has a job. But I want her to quit as soon as I find a place back here so we can raise a family here with all of you, my relatives. I'm staying down at Buffalo Bay Campground, he said, I got my own firewood and everything.

Will you teach me to be a medicine man like you? I seen an eagle out the bus window on my way here yesterday.

OVER THE NEXT FEW WEEKS this odd little fellow visited me almost daily. He was becoming a regular fixture in Red Cliff as well, walking everywhere he went, smiling and waving at complete strangers. I heard one of those damn Petersons sicced their dog after him just to be funny.

Your name will be *Bungi Boogat* (little fart), I said when he wouldn't stop bugging me for his Indian name.

What does that mean, he asked, and I said it means Soft Wind. Show me how it's spelled, he asked, so I wrote it down. When he came to visit me a day later it was written in magic marker on an old wrinkled t-shirt, just above Shaq slam dunking a basketball through the hoop.

Most of the time when he was at my place, he would just come to watch my TV. *SpongeBob SquarePants* was his favorite. After a while I noticed he didn't have a change in clothes so I took him down the road to St. Mary's Catholic Church to dig through the boxes of freebies, and he came up with a whole new wardrobe of wrinkled, stretched-out t-shirts and baggy-ass jeans, and a pair of flat-bottom tennies that probably cost two dollars new. At the same time we went over to the campground, and I talked my nephew who managed the place into giving Scottie a job being an all-around do anything in the campground, and after that day Scottie was the official haul firewood, cut it, put trash in the dumpster, clean out smelly shitters guy.

I see you have a new friend, one of the fat ladies in the tribal center smiled and winked at me the day I brought Scottie in to find out if he was indeed a Red Cliff tribal member. I gave her that look my crabby auntie was famous for and she almost burst out laughing. Turned out he really was a member of the tribe, so I told them he needed an emergency food voucher. A few days later I went there again with him to sign up for emergency housing.

Christ sakes, he's living in the campground, I said. Anyplace would be better than that. It's going to be getting cold soon. They got back to him in record time, two weeks, and told him he could move into an abandoned trailer house about a mile down on Blueberry Road.

I can call my wife, Jennifer, now and tell her I have a place, he said. I borrowed him my cell phone, and we went outside and stood on top of the septic mound where I get a decent signal, and dialed the numbers for him as well.

When he called her I overheard a woman hollering at him on the other end of the line about why in hell she hadn't heard from him in over two weeks. I got us a place, is all he could say, over and over, get up here. Get the bus money from your ma. And of course I was thinking, well, if Scottie is different, what is this Jennifer woman going to be like? It turned out his wife and baby would not show up for a month or more because she couldn't raise enough money for two bus tickets.

He'd been living in Red Cliff for about a month and coming up to visit me almost daily, and I wasn't getting sick of him, really. He was certainly a pleasant little fellow. Teach me the Indian word for this. Teach me the Indian word for that. It didn't matter. He'd forget it all before the end of the day.

Well, a few weeks back he didn't show when he said he'd be stopping by, and I almost missed him being there and all. The next day he didn't show, either, so I got in my pickup and drove on down to his new, old, formerly abandoned trailer to check on him only to find him hidden under a pile of tattered blankets and winter coats he'd rummaged somewhere. I'm sick, he said. So I hauled his ass out of bed and drove him over to the clinic.

They gave him a bottle of something or other and sent him on his way and told him to drink plenty of liquids and other nonsense like that he wouldn't remember, and we were soon on our way. However, they were on the ball enough to make a call to Milwaukee and have them fax important information from his medical file.

My niece works in medical records and, of course, she's bound by some secret pledge not to say anything, but she called me anyway when the records arrived and told me we needed to get his wife, Jennifer, up soon because Scottie was dying. There are no secrets here on the rez. Those of us who live here know that.

SCOTTIE, TELL ME WHAT you know about you being sick, I asked him the day after my niece called me.

I got lead poisoning when I was a baby. Paint chips, he said. I ate it like candy. He started laughing. That was pretty dumb wasn't it, he said. Eddie, I know I'm dumb. I been dumb forever. And I'm going to be dumb even longer. They tole me that lead made me dumb. Then when I got sick last spring they tole me I had some cancer, they're like little bugs that eat you up from the inside out the doctor says, and that mine has gone too far.

That's why I came to find you, he says. I need to know how to be an Indian before I go to the happy hunting ground.

And when he said that, I heard the traveling song we sing when we send a person's spirit off on their westward journey. Them spirits telling me my little friend wasn't long for this world.

Does your wife know? I asked.

No, he said. She doesn't need to know. I don't want her to worry.

But she will find out anyway, I say.

How's that if I don't tell, he says.

She'll find out anyway, I say. You need to tell her.

He says, okay, Eddie, and he's smiling all the while but I don't know how he can smile through all of this.

SCOTTIE CALLED HIS WIFE, Jennifer, the next morning and told her she needed to come right away and to be sure to bring the baby, Genevieve Mary. Get a bus ticket to Bayfield, he said. He'd walk into town and meet them. They needed to talk, he said. It was important.

His wife and daughter came just several days later. Jennifer, like Scottie, was like a child. Like two young ones playing house, only now they just had an old formerly abandoned trailer with saggy floors. He must have told her on the way from Bayfield because by the time they arrived at my place it looked like there had been a lot of tears shed. And that night Scottie and Jennifer were both on my cell standing up on top of the septic mound talking to his adoptive parents. They had listened to me when I told them they needed to tell all their loved ones. I watched their baby while they were on the phone, and later took her and my dog Chief for a walk, so Scottie and his wife could have some time alone. It was dark and cool and the air was filled with the sounds of frogs and crickets. The sky was filled with stars, and they wrapped around us like an alive blanket. We walked all the way down to the highway and back.

Many people have come to me to ask questions about their identity, their culture, over the years. And I've worked with them as they try to figure all of that out. None, however, have been like Scottie.

For all of them I leave a common message: If you want to learn, you will need to watch in a new way, a deeper way, I say. And you'll need to listen to more than just people's words, listen with all of your senses, and especially with your heart.

"Thank you, Uncle," many of them say to me. And maybe as a result I have many new, beautiful nephews and nieces now.

I asked Scottie if he and his family would stay with me a few days. It got pretty crazy in my little house, especially with the three of them there. We ate good, though, with Jennifer cooking up a storm and making trips to town for sweets. Chief was in his glory because he got plenty of table scraps and lots of attention. I haven't seen him run around and wag his tail like that in years.

After a few days, though, they moved to Scottie's place down on Blueberry Road. I went to see them every day, though, and to work with Scottie.

He's almost ready.

I take him with me when I do my work.

Like a couple of weeks ago I did a naming. One of the families in Red Cliff had asked if I would name their new daughter. It's a lot of work to do that, you know, because I have to really think about it hard, and dream about it. Those names come to me that way, in dreams. And there is a lot of responsibility in giving the name. In a way, I become a second guardian for the child. So, anyway, the family had prepared their house for a feast that day I named that little baby, with venison and wild rice and fresh baked *lugulate*—that's this pan bread we Ojibwe eat. I told Scottie he would be my helper at these things.

It's a long story, you know, the naming. But, anyway, I told the father and mother to take the baby from her *dikinagan* (cradleboard) and hand her to me. I took the little baby and held her close to my chest for a long time. In that way, it was like I was giving her a part of myself. That dream name I had for her passed over into her then. Then I held the baby out, and I spoke to her by her name, and held her out to her parents and introduced the new name to them.

This is *Mino-nodin-ikwezens*, I said, Good Wind Girl.

Sara and I, my wife, she's dead now, we never had children of our own. But I have daughters and sons all over Ojibwe country by having that gift from the Creator to give names to other people's children. They are like my own children, each of them.

Scottie came to me a day after we did the naming, and he offered me that tobacco and asked if I would name his baby, Genevieve Mary. I told him I had already dreamed her name.

When I go see him we talk about a lot of things. I have him tell me more about his life. He's trying to make sense of it, I can tell, and I feel that his sharing his life experiences with me will help him unravel it and put it together in a way that will make more sense to him.

But I can see we don't have much time now when I look in his eyes. Already, he's had to switch to stronger pain medication, and he is getting weaker and losing more weight.

I went to Lac Court Oreilles to see my friend *Mizaun* (Thistle), to ask him if he would come and do a sweat for my family. He said he would, and that my nephew Ronnie on my brother's side could be his helper, the fire keeper. That Ronnie is learning these things early on, you know. Someday it will be his turn. The circle will continue that way.

The night we had the sweat, that's when Scottie got the answers to all of his questions, I think. Because when we were sitting in the lodge, and passing the drum around, he said he still had questions about the why of his life.

Thank you, Mr. Creator, for bringing me here to Red Cliff to meet my Uncle Eddie so he could teach me how to be an Indian. See, I'm an Indian now. Ain't I so? Scottie said when it came his turn.

You sure are, we all said, almost in unison.

I reminded Scottie and the others who attended the sweat that evening that we humans are not perfect beings, and that we all stray from the Good Path. Then I told them in our language about what the Creator had intended for us in following that path.

I said the same thing I had told my nephew Ronnie just a few years ago when he was having trouble and trying to figure out his own place here on earth: There is a path to follow. It's hard, I know. I have failed many times myself. There is a certain way to live.

That we honor the Creator; that we honor our elders; that we honor our elder brothers, the plant and animal beings; that we honor women; that we keep our promises; that we be kind to everyone; that we be peaceful; that we be courageous; and that we be moderate in the way we walk through life.

The spirits of our family members who have passed on came in strong through that eastern doorway of the lodge that night. You could feel them all around us.

The Creator, you see, listens to all of us and watches over all of us. Even individuals like Scottie, and maybe even more so. We are all special in the eyes of the Creator. Each of us, including Scottie and all those like him, has our own unique gifts we bring into this world. Each of us has a purpose, a reason for being.

SOMEONE FARTED in the sweat that night and although he wouldn't admit it, we all knew who it was because he couldn't help but start giggling.

Did you hear the *boogat*?

I did, Scottie, I did.

A Place of Visions

When they had completed the mending of nets, the boy and his father put them into fish boxes and brought the boxes down to the boat. They tinkered with the boat's aging motor, the man explaining to the boy the numerous adjustments that needed to be made to ensure it could carry them safely out and back from a day on the big lake. He knew a time would come when Ron would need to know the old motor as intimately as he knew it. He knew as well that someday the boy would need to possess the skills to tear it apart and rebuild it and put it back together again. And he knew as well that someday the boy would also have to remove it and replace it with a new motor. So it was good that he got to know the boat and its workings now. And on this day as they bent over working on the motor, the father and his son talked and reminisced of other times and future times and times that would never be. Parts of the conversation were funny and laughter spilled out of the boat's cabin and carried over the lake. There were always the stories about the father and his brother, Eddie, the boy's uncle, when they were younger. Some of the stories began humorous and turned serious. Others were just the opposite. It was the father's way to use humor to teach. And on this day of humorous and serious stories, the father at one point called his son by his *Anishinaabe* Ojibwe name, *Beetanakwad* (Coming Cloud). Hand me the ratchet, *Beetanakwad*. I need a Phillips screwdriver, *Beetanakwad*. He would point with his lips to the needed tool. Point the *Anishinaabe* way. In a way it was a teasing. In a way it was serious. It was all of these things.

The boy asked his father about the name. He had done this before, and it was not unusual. Again the story was told. It was a story as old as the boat motor.

"One time when you were a little baby you got really sick. And we brought you into the rez clinic, and they gave you some medicine, but it didn't do you any good. You had a fever and diarrhea. I remember your mom and me we didn't know what to do. Mostly it was the diarrhea that bothered us. That can kill a baby because it dehydrates them. And you really stunk up the house with that diarrhea."

They both started laughing. Then the father's voice became serious and he spoke again to his son.

"And that went on for almost a week, and we were really getting worried. So one day your Uncle Eddie came over and he said something about maybe you should get an Indian name because in the old days the babies were always given Indian names so they wouldn't get sick. Now up until that point, we didn't know what else to do so we asked Eddie if he would give you a name. And he said he would.

"Now we didn't see him again for a couple of days but eventually he came over and said he had a name for you. And he reminded your mother that in the old days whenever someone was given their name there would be a big feast given by the family.

"Now, we was pretty broke back then—"

Ron had this mischievous look in his eyes and couldn't help but interrupt, saying, "So what else is new?"

The father smiled and unknowingly wiped some engine grease from his forehead. He continued the story.

"I wasn't working and your mom was cleaning a couple of houses for rich people over on Madeline Island and that was all the income we had, so all we had to eat was government commodities. So your mom opened one of those cans of commodity chicken, made some instant mashed potatoes and heated up a can of corn, and we had ourselves a feast.

"Then Eddie started to speak Ojibwe and English mixed, but mostly Ojibwe. Now, I know what he said but I can't tell it to you in Ojibwe. You see, I can understand our language, but I can't speak it fluently. Then I remember Eddie leaning over you and taking you by the hand and he said he was giving you a name. A name he had dreamed, he said. And he said it and told us it meant Coming Cloud. That name means you have great potential. That you have promise both as an individual and as a member of the tribe.

"So after that was done he had your mother put together a separate plate of food and he put some tobacco on it and took it out into the woods and offered it to the Great Spirit, or God or whatever he calls himself, or whatever. Now the next day you started to come out of it. Of course, Eddie says it was because you got that name. I think maybe it was something in the mashed potatoes."

They both laughed again.

The father then reminded the boy that in the giving of a name was the duty of the person to try to live the ideals in it and that it was also an obligation upon the part of parents to remind their children of the deeper meaning of the name.

"That's why you've heard this story so many times. You need to be reminded all the time. One of my jobs as a parent is to do that."

And the father was thinking when he said that about how many times he had told that story and how the boy had grown and changed since he was a little baby. When Ron was a baby he would be in the house in his Indian swing and one of his parents would push it and soon he would be asleep. Sometimes his mother would sing lullabies, the same ones her mother sang when she was a baby. Then on warm days he would be taken outside to show him the blue of the sky and the many forms of clouds. There he also came to learn the sounds of wind and crickets and birds. Although neither Ron nor his father knew it, for many thousands of years this was the way that Ojibwe children were taught the art of observation, and of listening. Not simply listening, but the deeper meaning of listening. Not simply observing the obvious, but searching for meaning beyond the obvious.

The father remembered all the children's stories he had told to this young man. Stories for the fun of it and stories for a deeper message. Stories to enhance the imagination. He remembered his own father saying that in the telling of a story the children also learned to dream. That dreaming was the first way of having visions. That there was purpose in it.

It was amazing to him that he had told the boy only once that he was never to utter his Indian name in *Ojibwemowin*. That was one thing Eddie told the boy as soon as he was old enough to understand. That for a person to speak their own *Anishinaabe* name was almost to be vain. That he was just a little boy when Eddie told him that and now he was a young man and never, never once had the boy said his *Anishinaabe* name. That he had never once heard him say *Beetanakwad*.

On that day after the pair grew bored of tinkering they stood on the pier and looked out over the lake. Less than a mile out was Basswood Island. It stood silent and beautiful and deep green against the blue of sky and water. And farther out were Madeline and Hermit and Oak islands. Just several hours earlier, the father had asked his son to come with him down to the boat to help him work on the motor. That is all he had told him. But he had meant many other things.

"Come with me, and we will share things. I will teach you the art of tinkering, a skill I have perfected from many years fishing with an old boat on the lake. We will spend this time together and get to know each other."

Before Ron and his father returned to their home, the boy looked over the side of the boat. The water was calm and he could see the image of himself in it. He gave himself a funny face. His image gave a funny face back. He looked at himself again. In the background was his father's voice.

"Ronnie. It's time to *majah* (leave)."

The boy looked at his image in the water.

"See you later, Coming Cloud," he whispered to himself.

THEY LOADED THE TOOLS into the back of the pickup and jumped in the cab. It roared to life, and they jerked their way up a steep incline, then down the highway past federally approved pastel government housing. Then off the paved highway and up the dirt road toward their house. The boy was thinking it was Friday and that on the following Tuesday he would be returning to school. Returning to school and no longer able to fish or mend nets or tinker with boat motors except for weekends. Thinking that even that would soon end because of the approach of fall and winter. He looked toward his father, wanting to hold onto this time forever.

"Dad, do you think we could go camping out on Basswood this weekend? You know, we haven't camped out there since spring, and pretty soon it'll be too cold to stay out there. Maybe we could hike to the other end of the island and camp near the old quarry. You remember . . . from there through the trees you can see Bayfield and Madeline. And if we camp there we won't have anyone else near us because if there are any tourists camping on Basswood, they will be staying right next to the pier. How about it? Just you and me."

The father looked toward his son and smiled. He knew that he had all kinds of work to do during the weekend. There were nets to be pulled and set again, and nets to be mended. There was some serious tinkering to be done in the work shed. He had also promised his wife they would spend an evening at the casino. But that could be done during the day and evening on Saturday.

"Sure, why not."

Because the father knew the time would come when a son would become an adult and leave his home. When he would no longer ask to spend time with his father. When the father would long for the company of his son.

So that afternoon after they returned home, they began the preparations to go camping, or to be correct, Ron made preparations to go camping with his father. He found the sleeping bags in the closet in his room, hidden under a pile of old clothes awaiting a trip to the Goodwill store. A kettle, frying pan, some utensils (camp utensils, consisting of a hodgepodge of bent forks, oversized spoons, and butter knives that were no longer straight), flashlight, matches, plastic garbage bag, a knife—all directly from the kitchen. A roll of scented toilet paper from the bathroom. And where was the tent, he asked. The father told him it was right where it was supposed to be, behind the back seat in the pickup truck. Now for the food. Some potatoes, eggs, a can of Spam and some coffee. Candy bars. Somewhere mixed in the rustle of food going into the pack was his mother reminding her son he was only going to be gone for one night.

"Remember to take the cell phone," said his mother, handing him the phone. "Just in case I need to tell you something."

But it was more than that. It meant take the phone just in case I want to talk to you. Just in case a freak storm blows in, and I wonder if you are okay. Just in case there is an emergency and I need to find Eddie to go out there and get you. Just in case I want to call you. Just in case I miss you.

So everything was stuffed into a pack and all of it together weighed enough to challenge any young weight lifter. When it came time to leave, the pickup fired up, and down the road they went, a father taking his son on an overnight adventure.

A young man hanging onto time forever.

They parked the truck next to the pier, and his father locked it up as if there was anything in it to steal. Ron pulled the pack out of the back of the truck and loaded it into the sixteen-foot aluminum boat they kept next to their fishing trawler, *The Megan*. His father handed him down an empty coffee can to dip excess water out of the back of the boat and indicated that today Ron would be the motor man. He said something about remembering to prime the motor this time and push the control to "start." Apparently this was something the boy had forgotten before, based upon past adventures.

After he had dipped out some rainwater, Ron pushed the priming bulb three times and pushed the control lever to start. It coughed and misfired several times. Then on the fourth pull it roared to life, proclaiming itself to the world with a pall of blue smoke. Soon they eased out away from the pier, then it was full speed out into the lake.

The ride over to Basswood Island was quiet and relatively calm. There was a light chop and only the hint of a breeze. They rode in silence across the water because to talk would be to interrupt the beauty of the ride. The wind in their hair. The slap of the water against the bow. Gulls. The approach of the island and fading away of mainland, almost as if they themselves were standing still and the rest of the world was both moving away and toward them at the same time. Halfway to the island and to the right was Madeline Island and the town of Bayfield. Off in the haze and to the south was Chequamegon Bay and the city of Ashland. To the left was the channel separating Basswood and the mainland. And through the channel, they could see Oak and Hermit islands. Sailboats. Fish trawlers. Pond nets. Behind them and fading into the hills, the Ojibwe village of Red Cliff. This was more than a simple boat ride. It was a journey that told the story of this place.

Soon they were approaching the pier on Basswood Island, and Ron nudged the boat up alongside it. He shut the motor down, and it coughed and sputtered and tried to keep running. His father jumped up and out of the boat and secured it with ropes at both the bow and stern. Ron handed the pack up to his father. He climbed out and stood on the pier, stretching as if he had just completed a long and treacherous journey. And he celebrated the end of this short journey the way all boys end all journeys.

"I need to pee," he said and headed into the bushes.

FROM THE PIER there was a trail that began with a steep incline and then meandered its way to the far side of the island. It was late afternoon and by some stroke of good fortune there were no other boats at the pier. That meant there were no other campers. They took the slow climb up the trail, stopping once to rest. At the top of the hill was a clearing, the island's camping spot, complete with a National Forest Service outhouse and several strategically placed fire pits. Here they turned and looked through the trees and down the hill toward the lake. Less than a mile away, resting in the mainland hills, was the village of Red Cliff. Two sailboats were headed toward the Bayfield slip under motor power. It was not uncommon for boats to run out of wind on late summer afternoons between Basswood and the mainland.

"How about camping right here?" Ron wondered aloud, thinking only of the weight of the pack, forgetting completely about camping near the quarry. But his father mumbled, "Nah," and they were off down the trail.

They continued down the trail for a half mile, taking turns carrying the pack. Soon they came to the long-abandoned brownstone quarry, overgrown with bushes and trees and moss. There on a large block of stone they sat to rest, and the father told his son about the place. About how early in the century some of the islands had been mined for the brownstone, the huge blocks shipped by steamer to Chicago and Duluth to become buildings. That now there was only a large overgrown cavity to show for it and how in time the earth would heal itself. And the father didn't say it but he was thinking about how time and circumstances had molded and changed the place. How their presence in the place at this time was just part of its story. He imagined an ancient sea pressing sand to stone. Of all the animals that had walked on it, eaten from it, and lived on it. He wondered about all the other people from other tribes and other times who had walked this trail, and who had lived and slept here. He had to ask himself, who would ever know that the stone of a building once nurtured life, or was once life itself? But he didn't say anything of what he was thinking because the boy was young and might not understand.

They continued the walk and soon came to the southeast side of the island. There they found a clearing and set up camp. It was a magical spot, close to the water yet hidden amongst the pines. It was not an approved National Park Service campsite, but they would make camp anyway. After all, his father said, the National Park Service had taken the land from the tribe against its wishes some years ago to establish their national lakeshore.

"This was Ojibwe land once. In fact, part of this island was once your grandmother's land. And as far as I'm concerned, it doesn't matter that they say we gave it up, or signed it away."

There was conviction in what he said, and more than a hint of resistance. Historical mistrust.

Ron's father set up the tent and unpacked their provisions. He sent the boy on a foray for dry wood, and Ron made several trips into the bushes and returned each time with large armloads of branches and twigs. Then he found several large dry logs, perfect for a late evening fire.

They made dinner, something with fried potatoes and Spam, smoke, twigs, and mosquitoes. Ron's father said it tasted French, and they both laughed. For dessert they each had a can of peaches out of the can. Dinner was followed by camp coffee.

"Stronger than jail coffee," his father said. There were secrets in what he said.

Then they sat and talked about the end of summer and the father told his son about the coming of fall. Of the storms that come during October and November and the times he had been caught in the storms on a leaky old trawler named *The Megan*, whose motor needed weekly tinkering to keep it running. Whose owner needed an occasional storm so he would have stories to tell a son.

"I remember one time we were out on the other side of Outer Island. Me and your Uncle Eddie. And that lake is so moody. When we had started out that day the weather was just fine. Sun was shining. Birds were chirping. Life was good.

"Then we got out there and started pulling nets and pretty soon all hell broke loose. Wind and then rain and that little boat was just bobbing up and down. Waves about ten feet high and nowhere to go.

"So we turned into the wind and started chugging to a protected area to sit it out, and of course the motor was missing and wanting to quit on us. And your mother was on the radio worried as hell and we were trying to keep the thing running and stay alive and talk to your mother all at the same time. And finally I said to your mom, 'Why don't you find someone else to talk to for a while?'

"Well the minute I said that, we were in a full gale."

There were other stories of storms and all of them had a happy ending because there was a father and his son around an early evening campfire. That is the proof of a happy ending.

When the father tired of fish and boat stories and the boy tired of asking questions, they sat quietly watching the fire. Now began a quiet time. A listening time. A watching time. The snap and sizzle of wood burning. Shadows created by its light. Warmth. A red and darkening sky. The first evening stars. The soft breeze that signals the beginning of night. A man and a boy staring into a fire the way people have looked into fires for many hundreds of thousands of years. Something old and almost primitive. They did this for a long time.

After some time they heard the sound of the cell phone, a country tune straight out of the memory of his father and mother.

It was the boy's mother asking what they were doing. Questions.

"Yup. Ah-huh. Hmmh. Oh, yah?" Ron began chewing on a candy bar and was trying to respond as best he could.

"Good night. Love you, too. You want to talk to Dad? Here, Dad."

Then it was the father's turn.

"Yup. Really. Geez. I'll see you tomorrow then, okay? Sure. Okay, then. Bye now."

Then she was gone for the evening. They were both glad she had called but did not share it.

Again just the man and his son.

"What time is it, Dad?"

"10:30."

"I think I'll go to bed."

INTO THE TENT. No sooner had the boy climbed into his sleeping bag and he drifted off to sleep. And to dream.

And in the dream he found himself on a river, sitting in the front of a canoe. He didn't know who was sitting in the rear, only the sense there was someone and that whoever it was did not constitute a threat. It was summer. Paddling to somewhere that was not important to the meaning of the dream. Into tree shadows and out into the sun. Around corners. Then to the right, a large tree with a barren top. And midway up the tree a young eagle, still dark in its colors. Another tree. Another young eagle. Ron noticed that maybe they could not fly away because they were too young.

Ahead of them. A crane standing in the water. Silent, as cranes are. As they approached, it rose in flight and disappeared down the river.

In the dream they continued the journey. Another bend in the river, and as they rounded it the crane was standing in the water and they approached within feet of it. But it rose again and flew downriver, around another bend. It was so quiet the only sound was the sound of its wings. This happened again. And again.

Another bend in the river. Small rapids. The crane in the water. This time as they approached it, the crane flew away from the river. It called out. Rare for cranes because silence was the usual way of the echo makers.

And it seemed he dreamed this the longest time.

Then the dream ended.

Gone. Like breath on a window.

That night he slept well past first light, and when he awoke his father was already up. The fire was burning and coffee was on. The father asked him how he slept. "Fine," he said.

"I had this dream last night. I can't really describe it. It was just so real."

And somewhere deep in the boy, deep in his ancestral memory, deep in the dreams that were passed on to him from the womb, from his grandfathers, a voice told him he was not to share this dream. Here in this place that was so simple and profound. A place whose story transcended time.

He noticed the way his father looked at him. An acknowledgement there are some dreams that one cannot share because to even to begin to describe them would be to destroy their magic.

They returned that morning to Red Cliff, a village of pastel-colored government housing, a burgeoning tribal infrastructure and with its new casino hotel that had yet to make any money. Up the hill above the village to a house built from rough lumber and garage sale windows. To a yard filled with modern reservation art and dead vehicles now used as storage sheds. A boy and his father. A father who has been teaching a son to fish and mend nets and tinker.

A son who has dreamed.

THE PEOPLE, THE WHOLE of the nation, had lived on the island for several hundred years. It was a bountiful and magical place because their canoes were within easy distance of the wild rice beds, as well as the hunting and berry picking regions of the mainland. The island was a safe place from enemies. It was the place where they had been told to live by their spiritual people, the whole tribe having followed the sacred megis *shell inland from the eastern ocean. Here on* Moningwanakining *(Place of the Yellow-breasted Woodpecker, Madeline Island) generations of families had raised children, fought wars, and survived in this land.*

And for many thousands of years the young of the tribe had sought visions, because visions gave meaning and purpose to living. Visions answered the "why" questions. And this is why in this time long past, a father had prepared his son for his vision. He had been preparing him for this since he was a young baby. First in the giving of his name, because in the giving of a name was conferred the ability to communicate with the spirit world. Because in the giving of a name was the obligation to pursue the ideals of the name.

Then when the boy was young his parents fostered in him the importance of observation and listening. He would be put outside in his dikinogan (cradleboard) on warm days and there he would observe the dance of life around him. He learned early in life to recognize the various birds and small creatures—squirrels, moles, and frogs. He learned early their languages and mannerisms. He learned the different sounds of trees and leaves, rushes and grasses and wind. He came to recognize the faces and voices of his father and mother, grandparents, uncles and aunties, and cousins.

And sometimes they would tell him simple stories, or they would sing to him stories. Sometimes the stories would be silent, pantomime about the animals he had come to know and the stories would tell of their purpose in the greater world. Although he did not know it, all of this was to sharpen his imagination, and to instill in him the ability to dream. Because dreams are a child's first visions.

As he grew older he would be asked to describe what he saw and heard in the external world. And in winter he would sit with his cousins and listen to the storytellers. There around the fire they would weave deeper meaning about life through parables, allegories, and songs. Some of these stories would be humorous and laughter would carry out of the wigiwams and over the lake. Some stories would instill fear because it is important that all men

*know fear. Then he would return to his home in the dark of night
and it would seem the stars would wrap around him like an alive
blanket. He would go to bed and when he grew tired of reliving
the stories in his imagination he would fall sleep.*

And dream.

*Now he had reached puberty, and his father had taken him
through purification ceremonies, to the lodge where his body
became cleansed by vapors. Then he took him to the place of visions, a nearby island whose collective mood and spirit, whose
quiet and aloneness was conducive to thought and reflection,
and to dreams.*

*Before they left they needed to make repairs to the boat.
Heated spruce pitch mixed with ashes to fill a small leak in the
birch canoe. While they did this, the father told his son stories.
He reminded him of the giving of his name and the importance
of living the ideals of the name. Then he handed his son a cedar
paddle. "You sit in the rear," he said. "You steer."*

*The journey to the island of visions was done in silence because
to speak would have disturbed the beauty of the place. The wind
in their hair. The slap of water against the bow of the canoe. Gulls.
To the south lay Chequamegon Bay. To the east and north the
deep blue and green of the other islands and the open water. Behind them, the smoke from their village on Moningwanikaning.
Together these things told the whole story of this place.*

*When they reached shore, the father took his son up a steep
incline and down a trail to a lodge he had constructed especially
for this journey. And he told him, "This is where you are to
think about your purpose here on earth. This is where you ask
the 'why' questions."*

*In this place the boy was left alone for four days, without
food. "Feed your spirit with your visions," his father had told
him. "There is purpose in it."*

For two nights he did not dream. On the third he had his dream:

He is standing in the water of a river. A canoe approaches. He recognizes himself in the rear of the canoe but does not know who is sitting in front. Another boy, one dressed in the manner of a tribe he does not recognize. In garments he does not recognize as the hides of any animal he knows. A boy who is not wearing moccasins but whose feet are nonetheless covered with a material he doesn't recognize. A boy with short hair. A boy who could be Ojibwe because he has that look.

Then he considers himself. How can I be in both places at the same time? *he asks himself.* How can I be both in the water and the canoe? *As the canoe comes near him, he rises out of the water in flight, above the trees. Below, he can see the winding of the river and the canoe on its journey.*

He lands in the water downstream. The canoe approaches again. He flies away. This happens again and again. There seems to be a purpose to it.

Finally, he flies away from the river to the big lake. Before he leaves them, he says something to his other self and the stranger in the canoe. Something in a language he has heard before but does not completely understand. Something about the past and the future. Something about things never changing and always changing.

To the islands. Below him on the largest island is the village of the people. He flies over it and lands in the water next to the island of visions.

The water is calm, and he can see his image in it. He turns his head sideways and looks deep into the image of a bird. A bird with a long beak and feathers and the deep and brooding

*eyes of one who has seen the past and the future. No longer just
a boy, but an echo maker.*
And a man.

ON THE FOLLOWING TUESDAY, Ron returned to school
for another year. The first day back seemed to drag on ex-
ceedingly slowly, and he counted his way through it hour
by hour. Finally the last class of the day, English, and the
teacher asked the students to write a paragraph about
something they did during the summer. One of those as-
signments that has been asked for years, maybe hundreds
of years. Maybe more.

There was an orchestrated chorus of voices, "But I can't
think about anything."

"You all must have done something this summer.
What about something you did this past weekend?" she
replied.

"Summer sucked." A mumble almost lost beneath a
rustle of paper, pencils tapping, squirming bodies, and
shuffling feet.

The boy was quiet and did not join in the bemoaning
of a summer lost. But for most of the class period, he sat
with a blank piece of paper in front of him. A slouching
eleventh grader too large for the desk he occupied. Wearing a Chicago Blackhawks cap on backwards, a pair of
imitation Girbaud's jeans and no-name basketball shoes.
Hair cut in a flat top, no tail. Straight as his mother
could cut it. Sitting in the back of the room where all the
reservation kids sat.

A boy who had dreamed.

In boredom he doodled on his paper, drawing a picture of a canoe and a large bird standing in the water. And he wrote a single sentence and turned it in before the echo of the final bell.

"This weekend I went camping with my dad."

Alice Crow Flies High

I came to Hull High School (Massachusetts) in September of 1984 as the learning disabilities teacher. I had two days to prepare before school was to begin. At that time I knew nothing of the Nantascots, pre-European residents of that Massachusetts, who were Lenape-speaking like my Ojibwe ancestors. Nantascot Beach, a long strip of sand and dunes that was Hull, was named after those ancient people. There certainly must have been times in the past when my Ojibwe ancestors and the Nantascot traded with each other, held council together. I wonder now if I would have looked differently at the community of Hull or of that place in general if I had known of those ancient people.

My first classroom was a small, windowless space in the lower level of the high school, between the boiler room and janitor's closet. All the real classrooms had long since been assigned to other "regular" classes. The floor of my new workspace was cement, painted a glossy gray, the walls a lumpy, uneven, government green. The room was lit by several caged 100-watt bulbs, and across the ceiling ran a large insulated heating pipe. Maybe the space had once housed the janitor's school supplies.

It surely had never been designed to be a classroom.

There was a hodgepodge of tables, several mismatched student desks, and a battered teacher's desk spun around backward in one corner of the room. A chalkboard was anchored to one of the walls with screws of various sizes. Any ordinary person, just by eyeballing it, would notice it wasn't level. Two boxes of dusty books sat on the teacher's desk. There was no paper, pencils, chalk, or erasers. I found a yellow magic marker in the desk drawer, without its cap, dry, abandoned.

The first thing I did was spit on a paper towel and wipe graffiti off one of the student desks near me. It read: "Go f--- yourself."

I smiled as I wiped it off, thinking that just a few years ago that could have been my writing on a desk somewhere. *My, how times have changed*, I remember thinking.

Then I sat on the edge of my new, old desk for several moments and wondered what in the hell I was doing there. But it didn't take me long to realize there was no turning back. This was where I was supposed to be, for whatever reason. So I got to work cleaning the place. I borrowed a broom and dust rag from the janitor's closet down the hall. Then I raided the teachers' supply room and scrounged some English grammar, composition and literature, math, and science books, books discarded years earlier that were awaiting the dumpster. After that I went to the principal's "first day back to work" luncheon and met my fellow teachers.

"Where did they put you?" one of my fellow teachers asked. When I told him, he laughed. I think I laughed too, just for the hell of it. I'm just saying. What in the hell else could I do?

"I think the football team stored some of their equipment there once," was the reply.

But the space I was stuck with was all I had, and it was mine, so I cleaned and scrubbed and devised lesson plans, in perfect Madeline Hunter fashion, just as I had learned as a student in the Teacher Education Department at U Mass, and got myself ready to face my first day of students.

On the first day, I had five students. Two were Hull locals. One was Vietnamese, and he had spent much of his early life in a refugee camp in Thailand and had been brought to California by a host family. His parents and extended families had somehow ended up in the Boston area, and then in Hull. Another student was Hmong, a tribal people from the highlands of Laos whose men had been recruited as fighters working covertly for the Central Intelligence Agency during the Vietnam War. With the fall of Vietnam and end of the war, some Hmong families had escaped certain persecution. The move from the mountains of Laos to America had suddenly thrust them from the Stone Age into the twentieth century.

And there was a dark, beautiful girl with raven hair. Her name was Alice Crow Flies High. She had moved with her family to Massachusetts from the Fort Berthold reservation in North Dakota. Her father had gotten a position as a job developer with the Boston Indian Council.

I was their new teacher, fresh and full of optimism. My five students were eager learners. After my very first day, I knew I was going to have one hell of a great time. In time, I was assigned three more students. And with each one I would smile at them and extend my hand in friendship and respect.

"I am Mr. Manypenny, but everyone here calls me Mr. D. You may call me Mr. D if you'd like.

"The 'D' is for my first name, Donovan."

That is how I would introduce myself to each year's group of arriving students. Most would remain in my class through their high school years or until they moved away. They would all attend regular classes as well—mathematics, sciences, business, art, and the vocational arts—but it was in my class at least one period a day, many times two periods, that they would all gather as one group. Here they shared camaraderie and all of the compassion and caring they were willing to accept from me, because somewhere deep inside me I remembered what it was like to be seen as different, or knew what it was like to be rejected or orphaned, or knew what it was like to be judged by my heritage rather than who I was as a person. To each I gave my utmost attention and concern.

"Chee, how are you doing in your other classes? If you bring me your daily work or homework, I'll do my best to help you when I can."

"Cindy, if you can stay after a bit this week, I'll work on that pronunciation with you."

"Xia, you need to practice speaking English every day. Every day, Xia. Not just here in this class. When you are with Mai and Yang, speak English. Go ahead and use Hmong when talking to Grandmother and Grandfather and Mother, but practice your English out of school with your Hmong friends. That is how you will learn English."

And of course I knew that if there was a teacher for English as a second language, some of my students certainly more appropriately belonged there rather than with me. But I did my best with them, taught them English, or at least I tried.

And Alice Crow Flies High was one of my favorites, I think, because she was, like me, Native.

"Alice Crow Flies High, you have a beautiful name. Do you know the story of your name? Can you tell me what it means?"

When I first asked her this, she just smiled shyly and looked down at the floor, and I told her that someday when she was ready she could tell me about her name.

By the end of my second year at Hull High School, I had started a Minority Student Club as a way of building a social community for some of my students and as a venue to educate the greater student body and community about the students and cultures. Membership was small in number, rarely over ten students in any given year. But as soon as the group became a recognized school club we began regular fundraisers so the club could hold their own social events. The most popular annual event became the ethnic cooking night, when the students would host a cooking clinic open to a public interested in learning how to make spring rolls and the like. A little known fact to the general public was that many of the students themselves didn't know much about cooking. Their mothers and grandmothers did most of the cooking in their homes. So they would gather up their family's favorite easy recipes and bring them to school, oftentimes cooking at the food show for the first time. One time one of my students of African-American heritage got the recipe he used out of the *Boston Globe*.

There were many occasions when I would find myself defending the students from teachers and administration and other students. On more than one occasion, other students would target one of them for taunting and abuse. Some of the harassment was simple bullying, but on other occasions the incidents had basis in a racial or ethnic bias. And of course much of it had to do with the fact that my students had learning disabilities.

One incident early on in my career seemed to define my role as an advocate for my students. It involved Alice Crow Flies High, who found herself the target of racial and sexual taunting, and of being called a "retard" by several of the school jocks. After a particularly difficult incident just before school one day, I came upon her sitting at her desk, crying.

"Alice, what's wrong?"

She looked the other way, saying nothing. She sniffled and wiped her nose off with the arm of her coat.

I sat down in the desk opposite her and for just a while looked at her. I let her become comfortable with my presence.

"Tell me, Alice. What's wrong? Maybe I can help."

"I don't want to talk about it, Mr. D."

"I understand. But the only way I can help is if you tell me what's wrong. Can you do that for me, Alice?"

Her hands went to her lips, and then she wiped the tears away from her eyes again. Finally, she spoke.

"They call me a whore, a squaw. They say we eat dogs. They stand all around me. Some of them try to touch me. I don't know what to do. I tell them, leave me alone. They don't listen. They just laugh. They call me a retard, too."

I reached over and touched her hand. For just that moment, memory came and sat down beside me. Of me as a little boy, standing in a playground surrounded by a group of town boys.

"Hey, Chief."
"I ain't no chief."
"Then you just a regular honest Injun?"
"I ain't no Injun, either."

"You know, Alice, when I was a little kid, I was teased horribly in one of the schools I was in because of my Native heritage. I'm Ojibwe, you see. You know that?"

She looked at me.

"I wondered what you were," she said to me. Then she smiled, just a little. Sometimes, you know, there is an unspoken recognition, an acceptance, when we Native people talk.

I continued. "It was terrible, I remember, and I fought back. Now I'm not telling you what to do in your case, but I would like to help if you'll let me. No one should have to come to school and be treated like that. No one. I can help you, Alice. I want to help you. Will you let me do that?"

Alice sat there with her head down, still in tears.

"Let's go see the principal, okay?"

She nodded in acknowledgement, and we went up to the principal's office.

As we approached the receptionist's office, I again reassured her. "Things are going to be all right now, okay?"

After hearing her story, the principal called the perpetrators in one by one to get their stories. There was a reason for him doing this. They would eventually turn against each other using the "he said, she said" routine. He figured right, and they did implicate each other. As a result, four of the boys were suspended from school for three days

111

each and were not allowed to play in the football game that Friday. The decision was unpopular with the athletic director and coach, who lost four of his varsity players as a result of the decision. It was also unpopular with the boys' parents, several of whom called the principal to complain that their boys had never, ever before been in trouble in school, and that the punishment had been too harsh. "Boys will be boys," one of their mothers had said. One of the parents even called a school committee member, who in turn called the superintendent, who called the principal and inquired what was going on. But in this case, the principal stuck to his guns.

I suppose, however, I paid a price for helping Alice. Some days after the boys had returned to school, I found the driver's side mirror to my car had been broken off as it sat in the faculty parking area, and there was a large scratch all along the driver's side where someone had keyed it.

I could not have imagined back in 1969, when I was somewhere in the middle of the Vietnam War, that someday I would be teaching some the children of refugees of that war, being their advocate. Sometimes I have asked myself if my decision to teach students with special needs was somehow unconsciously linked to my experience there, to the times I stood by and watched the needless suffering of Vietnamese civilians, people who were dark-skinned like me, who suffered the same atrocities as my ancestors. Maybe unconsciously I had decided that someday I would do something to try to make up for it, without ever realizing it.

And to be a teacher to Alice Crow Flies High, who was Lakota and a long way from Fort Berthold, North Dakota, and the rolling sea of grass and wind.

After that incident with the jocks and Alice, she opened up to me. She told me that back home her family had horses.

"I miss my horses," she would say to me in her reservation sing-song English voice. Then she would tell me of riding them across the rolling hills of her reservation.

Alice was receiving special education because she had difficulty with reading and recalling. So besides the regular reading materials I was able to scrounge, I went looking for materials that had something to do with her Lakota heritage, and books about horses.

She was in my classroom for three years, until she graduated in 1987.

I still remember at graduation she wore an eagle feather given to her by her grandmother, who came all the way out from North Dakota to see her get her diploma.

The years have gone by, and me, I'm still teaching at Hull High School. I still love teaching, still love working with students with an array of learning disabilities.

From time to time, Alice Crow Flies High sends me a card to let me know of important times in her life—when she got a degree in social work from the University of North Dakota and started work for her tribe's human services department; of her marriage; of her first child.

"Mr. D.," her cards always begin.

The last time I heard from her was about five years ago. She sent a picture of her oldest daughter, a spitting image of Alice when she first came into my classroom so many years ago.

And she was sitting tall on a horse.

In the Creator's Eyes

I can't really articulate everything that transpired to send me on this journey, but when I turned fifty I went to find things about my Native heritage. You see, I'd been living with my grandparents because my mother ditched out on me soon after I was born. My grandparents died just a few months apart when I was ten years old, and I was fortunate to be adopted instead of spending the rest of my childhood being bounced from foster home to foster home.

Soon after they took me in, we moved from my birthplace in northern Wisconsin to Massachusetts, where I was raised by my new parents, who couldn't have any children of their own. They were white Irish like most of the people living in Dorchester at the time, and me, I was brown as can be. Well, growing up there with all those poor Irish kids, I got teased a lot and called all kinds of racially derogatory things, especially the "N" word, but no one ever called me a redskin or wagon burner, or all those other names that Native people are called in a derogatory way. Anyway, I just lived my life away in the Boston area all those years without too much thought about my birth mother or whether I had any brothers or sisters, or anything about my Ojibwe heritage. Along the way I became a special educator, teaching young people with learning disabilities. Then at fifty I went in for my annual physical and found out I was diabetic, and the doctor said that certain ethnic groups are almost predisposed to it. "Like what ethnic groups," I asked, and he rattled off the list, and one group mentioned was Native American. Me, all along I'd been living like a white guy painted brown, so being referred to as something "other" was new to me, at least as an adult. Anyway, to make a long story short, that led me to thinking about my origins and birth mother and all. And I suppose being diagnosed as a diabetic caused me to think about my own mortality. Pretty soon all I could think about was going to northern Wisconsin, Red Cliff, where I was born.

My adopted mother and father had been good to me and had treated me like their own. And, of course, when I was old enough they had reminded me where I was from originally and that I was Ojibwe. I knew enough to keep that in my memory banks.

Guess I'm just a late bloomer, or having a late mid-life crisis or something. I started reading all about my Ojibwe heritage in books I searched on the Internet and ordered through Amazon—*Ojibway Heritage* and *Ojibwe Ceremonies* by Basil Johnson, *The Mishomis Book* by Eddie Benton Banai. Reading the books just gave me a thirst for more knowledge. Through reading I learned that my Ojibwe ancestors had at one time lived on the Atlantic coast, but had migrated westward over a thousand years ago because of a series of prophecies.

I wish I could explain it, but I just kept thinking about "home," a place I had never seen since I was a young boy, but wanted to know more about. So this past summer I just started the long drive back to Red Cliff, Wisconsin, where I was born. My wife couldn't go because she had already burned her vacation time, but she gave me her blessings.

I decided to take the northern route, to follow the path of the ancient Ojibwe migration, to see each of the stops made by my ancient ancestors—Montreal, Detroit River, Manitoulin Island, Sault Ste. Marie, Duluth, and finally Madeline Island. I guess I felt that if I walked in the same places as my ancestors, and saw what they saw, sort of, then it would help me understand more about them, and ultimately, more about me.

My first stop was in northern Maine, a Passamaquoddy reserve. I had read an article a few months back in the *Boston Globe* about the place, and about a Native man, Wayne Bishop, a blind man who was a teacher of the language, history, and culture at the reserve school, as he put it, "so traditional knowledge could be passed on down the generations." And I thought maybe he could lend me some insight into my own journey. So that made me decide, what the hell, I'll stop there and see if he'll take some time and talk to me.

Indian Township is a six-hour drive north of Boston, deep in the woods and lake country of northern Maine. I arrived there mid-afternoon. I was far enough north to see my first "Moose crossing" road signs. I laughed to myself when I first saw it, because I have this big dude of a neighbor who lives the next door down in Hingham that sign would be perfect for. As I pulled into the village, one of the first buildings I noticed was an old wooden school, with a parking lot filled with cars and children playing out in the playground. A school, I was thinking, a familiar place to an old teacher like me.

I made my way to the principal's office and introduced myself to the receptionist, a young Native woman. I told her why I was there, that I was a teacher and where, and that when I noticed the school I figured it was probably the best place to stop and ask.

"I'm interested in learning more about my Native heritage and thought maybe you could let me know how I could get in touch with the man the *Globe* profiled a few months back, the one who teaches language, history, and culture here. I'm Ojibwe, you see, but I was adopted out young and never learned anything about those ways. So now I want to know more, and I thought maybe this was where I could begin, by talking to him."

"Wayne is down in the lunch room. He teaches our summer Passamaquoddy language and culture. Just go down the hall that way," she said, pointing with her lips.

That was a first. I hadn't seen anyone point with their lips before.

The elderly man the receptionist referred to only as "Wayne" was sitting at a lunch table having coffee when I entered the room. He appeared to be about seventy years old and had thick salt-and-pepper hair tied back in a tail. He was surrounded by a group of five or six children, all Native. They were laughing, and I could tell right away how much the children liked and respected this man.

When I walked over and introduced myself, he seemed eager to talk to me. He turned toward me, his blind eyes facing me, and I reached toward him and grasped his hand. He shooed the children away.

"Go on outside and play now, children. The bus will be here any minute," he told them, waving the white cane he kept alongside his knee and laughing gently.

"Goodbye, Uncle," they said. Each of them came to him and gave him a hug.

When they were gone he led me outside to a picnic table, then lit a cigarette and sat down.

I didn't really know why, but I felt very comfortable with the man. So comfortable I just started jabbering away. I told him my life story, about vague memories of when I was a small child in Red Cliff, Wisconsin, about my grandparents, and about my adoption and moving to Boston.

"Now I'm headed back home to see where I came from. I don't know what to tell you, but something is just calling me back there. It's just something I've got to do."

Then I told him what little I knew about the time the Ojibwe had lived on the East Coast, and of their migration west. The man listened to me as I talked. He hadn't said much at all, intent only on hearing my story.

Then I finally shut my trap he started talking, and I, the teacher, became the learner. He said he had gone to a Native language gathering a few years ago in Tama, Iowa.

"I speak my language and I teach it here to these children. Anyway, when I was at this conference I heard others speak their languages—Cree, Ojibwe, Odawa, Mesquakie, Pottawatomi. I could understand a lot of what they were saying," he said, "and, for the most part, they could understand me. We're all related, you know."

"You know," he continued. "When you Ojibwe went west, we sent you there. We stayed here."

Then we both laughed. I was thinking that was the likely story coming from those who had stayed.

"You're full of it," I said, laughing, teasingly.

"You'll never know," Wayne replied, also laughing, his voice gentle, knowing.

(There was one group who supported the migration but who pledged to remain at the eastern doorway and care for the eastern fire of the people. They were the Wa-bun-u-keeg' or Daybreak People.)

The elderly man impressed me like few men I had ever met before, but I couldn't explain why. Maybe it was the way he conducted himself, with certainness and a quiet dignity. I had opened myself up to him like I'd had known him for years, like he was my trusted friend, a respected teacher.

Wayne told me that he'd lived in Indian Township most of his life, and that he also served as a member of the tribal council.

"I'm the honest one," he said and laughed when he said it. Then he told me more about himself.

His children were grown, but they all lived on the reserve. His wife and he were raising two of their grandchildren because one of their daughters was unable to raise them on her own.

"Drinking," is all he said.

"The grandkids speak our language, though. All of them." He spoke proudly when he said that.

"My house is always full of grandkids and nephews and nieces, and my grown children, all coming and going. It can be a busy place. But I wouldn't trade it for anything."

We talked that afternoon for a long time. Then he stood.

"How far are you going to drive tonight, my friend?" Wayne asked me.

"I was just going to go down the road as far as Calais. Going to head up toward Montreal tomorrow."

"Well, rather than have to spend money on a motel room, why don't you stay with us tonight?"

I was quietly pleased to be asked. "Are you sure?"

"Of course. Now, let's get out of here. I'm done for the day."

I followed Wayne back into the school and down the hall to his classroom so he could pick up his things, then down the hall and out the door, the tapping of his cane echoing off the walls as we walked. There I led him out to my car and we drove down a dirt road a few miles to his place, an old farmhouse nestled in a grove of trees.

Wayne's description of all the activity in his home was right on. It was a busy place, with the phone always ringing, kids coming and going, and sons and daughters visiting. Wayne's wife had a fresh pot of coffee on and cookies and other snacks for their company to munch on. She seemed a lot like Wayne, happy, content. I felt immediately at home, like I was family, and, thus, I knew why the Bishop home was always filled with their loved ones. Everyone who came through the door felt good there. Theirs was a joyous place.

When it was time for dinner, Wayne's wife and a daughter and several daughters-in-law all pitched in and took over the kitchen. When it was ready, the food was all set out on the kitchen table, buffet style.

She handed her husband and me each a plate and fork.

"You two eat first," she said. Then she looked toward me to explain.

"Elders always eat first in this home."

There was plenty of it. Boiled potatoes, macaroni and cheese, hot dogs, goulash, Kool-Aid, bread, government cheese, government peanut butter. For dessert there was white cake with chocolate frosting, washed down with plenty of strong coffee. I filled my plate several times, eating while sitting in a living room chair, balancing the plate on my lap, with my coffee cup resting on the floor beside me, all the while one of Wayne's grandkids was sitting alongside him on the floor, looking up at him.

When dinner was complete, the house slowly began to empty. We talked. I told Wayne and his wife, Lorraine, about my wife and daughter, my work as a special educator, and about growing up and living in and around the Boston area.

"I went for a semester to BU (Boston University)," Wayne told me. "But I got so damn lonely for home I flunked out and came home. So I finished up down at Orono."

We talked until nearly midnight. Wayne shared his knowledge of the history of his tribe. I shared what little I knew of the Ojibwe people from the reading I had just completed. We became immediate friends.

I was curious, of course, about how Wayne was treated in his community as a blind person. Surely from what I saw in the eyes of his students, adult children, grandchildren, and wife, he was a person who was deeply loved, respected, and admired. And even I, who had not spent time around a Native elder since I was a young boy, sensed his gentle spirit. So I gathered my courage and asked him.

"Wayne," I said, hesitantly, "what is it like as a non-sighted person, as a teacher, and as a Native person, in the school where you work and the community in which you live?"

He was sitting in his rocking chair, his white cane resting at his knee, and he reached for it and rubbed it and licked his lips, and thought. Then he finally talked.

"You know," he began, "I never had any trouble with people here. Never. I never did. Other places I suppose people judged me differently because I am blind."

And he told a story about when he went to Orono for the first time and overheard someone whispering about "that blind injun."

"Here," he said, "I've never ever felt any less, or been treated any less. Our ancestors, you see, they had people like me back in them days. I heard about this from my grandparents."

He smiled gently.

"In the old language, the language before the Europeans," he said, "there was no word for blind. There was no word for deaf. We are all equal in the eyes of the Creator."

I WAS GIVEN THE GRANDKIDS' room to sleep in for the night, and when I finally made my way into bed I drifted right off to sleep. I slept better than I had in a long, long time.

Wayne was sitting at the kitchen table having coffee when I arose the next day.

"Did you sleep well last night, my friend?"

"I slept like a baby."

Lorraine had already prepared our breakfast. Oatmeal, toast, bacon, scrambled eggs. The coffee was appropriately strong.

I knew it was time for me to hit the road. Wayne needed to get to work, and I had a long drive ahead of me. After we had finished our meal, I stood and brought my plate over to the sink and put it in the soapy water.

"I want to thank the both of you for having me in your home. Your children and grandchildren are very lucky to have the two of you. You both made me feel very special. I feel so much at home here. I'm beginning to see things and think ways I haven't done before."

And I was thinking how it took a gentle, blind man to open my eyes, to point me in the right direction, and to help me along the way in my journey.

Wayne put his hand on my shoulder. "Maybe the next time you come around we'll have some fresh moose meat to fry up."

Then he laughed, and so did I.

"Uncle . . ." I began to inquire of him.

He pursed his lips and said, "You see, we Passamaquoddy are still sending you Ojibwe on your way."

Maggie

My birth certificate reads that I was born on February 27, 1951, at the Hennepin County Medical Center in Minneapolis, mother Genevieve Ann Manypenny, father unknown. I remember I had a hard time finding an original copy of that certificate once I decided to go looking for it. I was eighteen years old at the time. At first I went to the Hennepin County offices. After all, that's where I was living at the time, and I didn't know any other place to look. Well, they didn't have it, which made me wonder. Then someone told me that maybe I could find it in the Minnesota Department of Public Records over by the University of Minnesota Hospital, just off Washington Avenue, so I went over there. Ten dollars later and I had my own certified copy. Apparently, illegitimate births are stored at the state office, not at the county of birth. And that made me ask, what if someone didn't know that she or he was illegitimate? How would the person know where to look? And when they found out, that would be one hell of a way to find out, wouldn't it?

I knew things were going to be screwy early on because I grew up being bounced from foster home to foster home, group homes, and for a while, anyway, juvenile centers. It all made sense later on when I was older and the social worker told me my mother signed me away right there at the hospital right after I was born. The first home I remember was up in Brooklyn Center. I started kindergarten there—that's why I remember. I was living with this family. They were all blond-haired, blue-eyed Scandinavians, true-blue Minnesotans for sure, don'tcha know. I shouldn't make fun of them. They were really very nice people. They had two boys of their own, both a couple of years older than I was. They were real nice to me, at least that's what I remember, and I got along at school reasonably well, except for teasing from some boys who called me "squaw baby" and things like that once in a while. I remember once I told my teacher about it. After all, I was her pet, sort of. She told me to tell them that sticks and stones may break my bones, but words would never hurt me. I didn't like her as much after that.

Anyway, I stayed with that family until sometime in the middle of the third grade. Then the man got transferred in his job or something, and there I was being sent to a temporary foster home. That was a nightmare, I remember, because I had really gotten to like the lady in the Brooklyn Center home. And the new foster mother would get mad at me sometimes and pinch me hard until I had bruises all over the back of my arms. School wasn't going too hot, either. I started having a lot of trouble with reading and math. At first I got put into Title I, or whatever it is called, for supplemental reading and math. When that didn't work they did an assessment and I ended up in an LD (learning disability) room, where I spent two hours every day. And of course even then as a young kid I noticed that most of the other kids in that room were brown like me, and most of the "regular" kids at the school were whiter than ghosts.

From there I ended up in Wayzata for a couple of years. Those people were rich, and I was the only child in their home. The woman there bought me new clothes all the time, and we went on trips to Disneyland in California, and to New York to visit their relatives. School wasn't good, though. I was in another special education room and having a heck of a time getting things to sink in. Looking back at it all, I suppose I had a lot going on in my life, and all that just made school hard to deal with.

I loved it there in the foster home, though. But the couple got in some awful fights sometimes, and one time the man didn't come home after one of their big fights. I remember I begged my foster mom to take him back because I knew that if they broke up, I would end up being sent to another home. Well, they broke up.

By that time I was in the sixth grade and getting tough as nails. I ended up being sent to another foster home somewhere near the West Bank of the University. The couple that took me both taught at the U. Their kids were all grown up and moved away. They had one other foster girl, Marilyn. These people were okay, I guess. But I remember getting dragged to all kinds of boring adult things—art exhibits, guest lecturers, symposiums, poetry readings, and the like. Now that I'm an adult, I'd die to get the opportunity to go to any of these types of events. We never get anything resembling that here in Red Cliff.

Well anyway, Marilyn, the other foster girl there, was in the seventh grade. She introduced me to smoking and stealing candy and other things from stores. I'd act like the decoy, asking the clerk where things were, while Marilyn helped herself to whatever she could fit in her pockets. We were pretty good at it, as I recall. At least, we never got caught. Marilyn was always talking about running. She had sisters and brothers in other foster homes scattered all over the Minneapolis-St. Paul area, and she must have missed them like crazy. She wanted to go home to her mom, even though she told me that her mom drank a lot.

At school I was still receiving special education in reading and math and I suppose that it helped. Of course, I noticed most of my schoolmates in that room were brown people like me and I began to resent it.

Back in the foster home I was a good follower, so the night Marilyn decided it was time to run, I tagged along. We took buses to South Minneapolis to her old neighborhood and found her mom and boyfriend, and a bunch of other people, all drinking it up. It was scary. I remember I didn't want to stay. But I did anyway, for a couple of days. Then her mom sobered up and said that she could get into trouble for having me there and that I would have to go. So there I was out on the street. Twelve years old. Luckily, the police picked me up just a couple of hours later walking down Cedar Avenue on my way back to the West Bank.

The U couple, of course, wanted nothing to do with me anymore, so I ended up getting put in my first group home in Eden Prairie. That wasn't too bad, actually, because I got to be with a bunch of other girls. I stayed there for two years and then I ran again. Don't ask me why. It was really stupid. Things were going okay there for me at the time, and in school. A couple of us ran together that time. We hitched rides up Highway 61. One of the girls had relatives living near Duluth, she said, and we could stay there. That turned out to be a crock. The highway patrol had us in the back seat of a patrol car just out of Carlton, Minnesota, two days later. One of the other girls and I had decided to hitch back to the Cities. That little escapade put me in the juvenile center.

From there, things were kind of a blur. I bounced around in temporary or permanent placements, a few other group homes, and in and out of the juvenile center. I was hanging out with some pretty rugged kids, so school wasn't going great, either. I'm thinking I was in special education from the third grade on all the way through high school. That and skipping school and not doing homework, not studying, all that kind of crap sort of added up to a pretty dismal school transcript.

But I grew up or something, all of a sudden, when I was seventeen and entering the twelfth grade. I promised my social worker I was changed, and she believed me for some reason. She found a nice, older, single lady to take me in for my senior year. She had a nice big house just off Cedar in a mixed neighborhood. Her name was Martha.

She was the closest thing to a mother I ever had.

Looking back now, I feel fortunate I survived those growing-up years. I could have easily ended up getting killed the way I lived. Drinking, drugs, you name it. But Martha was just this kindly old lady, and I don't know how else to put it, but I didn't want to disappoint her. So I buckled down and starting going to all my classes. I quit hanging out with the losers and found a couple of decent friends. I even had a nice boyfriend who picked me up and took me to cinemas, just like in the movies. Shit, every other boy I'd known before had just tried to get me drunk so he could get in my pants.

I graduated from Minneapolis South in 1969, at eighteen years of age. My diploma had an asterisk on it, I found out later, to signify that I was in special education. Here, I thought I was special for another reason. Martha said I could stay with her as long as I wanted, even though the county ended the foster care checks. I stayed with her until I was twenty-two. By then I was paying her some rent to help with the bills. She got sick, though, and died of some kind of viral infection my senior year of college. Her funeral was really sad because she really didn't have any family. I was it.

There had been a Native program at South High when I was there, and I hung out there once in a while because I always knew I was Native. I just didn't know much about my Native heritage, and hanging out there was my way of finding out. Anyway, the Native counselor asked me if I was interested in going to college, and I told him I'd never really thought about it. I wasn't sure I could handle college, being in special education and all. He said a lot of money was available, and I would probably get a free ride if I packaged it right with my financial aid.

I remember him asking me, "So what rez are you from?"

And I said something like, "Franklin Avenue." You see, all the Native people in Minneapolis, it seemed anyway, lived on Franklin Ave.

"No, I mean, where are you enrolled?" he asked again. I had to tell him I had no idea.

So that's what got me to looking for my birth certificate. I found it but didn't follow up on finding out what rez I was from. That was about it for the next four years, because college preoccupied my time.

I suppose having spent most of my school years thinking I was dumb, and being in special education classrooms, college wasn't even on my radar. But the Native counselor talked me into it somehow and I ended up applying and getting accepted at Metro State in St. Paul. My grades weren't that good in high school, and my ACT scores were pretty dismal. Maybe they were trying to meet some racial quota or something and that's how I got in. They had a good program to support us Native students, though, and I went to the college's access center to help me out with academics, particularly with writing. They found me a good editor, and that seemed to make a lot of difference. I did pretty well there, all things considered, graduating in 1973 with a teaching degree in early childhood special education. I suppose because I had spent most of my schooling receiving special educational services myself, this was something I knew well. In my heart, though, I wanted to go back into schools as the teacher. And as a Native teacher, I wanted to see if I could do something to help young students of color in special education, be their advocate, their voice. I wanted to do something about the high placement rate of students of color in special education as well.

I got my first teaching job at an early childhood center near Chicago Avenue and Lake Street, in the heart of the ghetto, and worked there for six years. And I fell in love and married a white man I first met at an early childhood conference in Rosedale. That didn't last. In less than six months I was divorced, wounded, relieved, and I intended to be more cautious the next time around. That is a whole other story, though.

Like so many Native people living in Minneapolis, I attended pow-wows and other social gatherings at the Minneapolis Indian Center. I still didn't know if I was an enrolled tribal member or not, or where I really came from. But I wondered about it, more so as the years passed. So one day I asked a social worker friend who worked there how I might go about finding out, and she said if I had my birth certificate she would help me begin the search. She helped me write letters to the Social Security Administration to see if my birth mother, Genevieve Manypenny, was still alive. If she was, she could be identified through her social security number. She told me to visit the area office of the Bureau of Indian Affairs in downtown Minneapolis. They had me contact all the agency enrollment offices within their jurisdiction, which included Minnesota, Wisconsin, and Michigan.

By now it was 1980. Then one day I got a letter from the Ashland Agency saying they had a Genevieve Ann Manypenny on the rolls at Red Cliff Reservation in Wisconsin. The letter also indicated she was deceased.

I was so disappointed when I read that, I just sat down and cried. But my social worker friend said, "Hey, you might still have a whole family up there in Red Cliff. Let's go see."

So the next weekend we got in my car and drove up to Red Cliff. It was the middle of October and colder than hell there, and I remember thinking, *who in the hell could ever live in this godforsaken place?* We stayed in Bayfield mostly because it catered to tourists.

That Sunday we drove back to Minneapolis and I figured there was no looking back. But some kind of invisible ancestral hook must have been pulling me back all the while, because a few months later I saw a job posting for a Head Start ECSE (early childhood special education) teacher at the center in Red Cliff, Wisconsin, and before you know it my application was in the mail. A month later I was there again for my interview, and two weeks after that I was there again looking for a place to live.

I met Ron, my husband, just a week after I'd moved here. He came into the Head Start building with his brother Eddie, who was one of our cultural aides. I think Ronnie and I fell in love the minute we laid eyes on one another, and there was no turning back fate so far as we were concerned. Before the school year was out, I was barefoot and pregnant, and standing in our kitchen cooking fry bread.

In the meantime, I took my birth certificate to the tribal council and proved my ancestry and became an enrolled member of the tribe.

And I've been here ever since.

This place is so much a part of my soul I will never leave it.

THE EARLY CHILDHOOD center here never had a Native person as a licensed teacher before, let alone an ECSE teacher. And I take my work seriously, particularly with regards to assessment and being careful so as to not attach the "special ed" label to these young ones unless they truly need the services. There are so many issues from what I see on why so many minorities, Native people, end up in special education. From my perspective, at least, much of the problem is that fuzzy area of race, socio-economic status, and disability. At least from my perspective, race plays its hand in the decision-making process all along the way, from initial referral to placement. If I were to pinpoint the problem to one area in particular, it would be assessment.

So I am always shooting off my big mouth when I think the other teachers are shirking their teacher duties and just trying to pawn young ones off into my classroom because they can't deal with them for some reason or the other. So at least here at our center we are careful in making a placement unless it really is necessary.

That, of course, isn't the case when it comes to the local public school. There, all kinds of Native students end up in special education classrooms. And when I found that out, I ran for the Indian parent committee and was elected. I use that as my pulpit to raise hell with the school system. Here they are with 800 or so kids in the schools, over seventy percent of them Native, and nearly all the kids identified for special education are reservation kids. So when I had a chance to talk in front of the school board last week I let them have it with both barrels, and it really got their ears perked up because I let them know that we are going to be watching them. I don't think they were use to hearing a Native person spit back all that educational jargon to them like they've been dishing out to us all these years to confuse us, so it was fun to watch them squirm. Just a summary of what I said, straight from the school board minutes:

"Aniin Neeji Bemaadizing. Makaday Migizi Equay nin dizinikaz. Maggie Manypenny nindizinikaz zhaganashshimong. Hello, fellow human beings. Black Eagle Woman is my name. Maggie ManyPenny is my English name.

"I'm here tonight to talk with you about our Native kids and special education. I suppose I have a special place in my heart for these kids. You see, I was identified and placed in special education as learning disabled from the third grade on all the way through high school. I suppose in a way maybe I belonged there, for at least some of those years, but now that I'm older, I wonder if maybe I just didn't need a jumpstart. And now that I'm a teacher, a Native teacher and special educator myself, I want to advocate and ensure that none of our reservation young ones ends up in special classrooms unless they truly belong there. And likewise, I want the ones who really need it to receive the services they deserve.

"I want to say from my perspective the reasons so many of our Native kids end up in special education. The reasons have to do with a variety of things: of coming from families that are poor, where there is little in the way of reading or enrichment materials in the home; of events in their home life that interfere with their schooling; of the decisions made by teachers, the vast majority being white teachers, mind you, and white administrators, making decisions that result in a special education placement; of teachers and administrators who know little if anything about Native kids, teaching Native kids, and have little if any knowledge about our language, history, and culture; administrative policies (discipline, curriculum, instruction) that favor mainstream (white) kids over our Native kids;

pressure to put our kids in special education because of the state tests and graduation standards. Mostly, however, I think the issue lies in subjectivity in the psychological and assessment practices that are used to determine placement. Somewhere in these practices the race card is exposed. Why else do the vast majority of the kids in special education classrooms have brown skin? Why else is there such a high incidence of Black, Hispanic and Native kids in SLD (specific learning disability) and EBD (emotional behavioral disorder) placements all over this country?

"You people can't fool me and tell me that so many of our Native kids belong in these placements. I've been there. I am there."

You should have seen that school board room when I sat down. You could have heard a pin drop it got so quiet. And when I sat down I was so emotional my voice was cracking and I started crying, and my mind was flashing all the things from my life experience that led me there to that room, that night.

So I'm going to watch those people like a hawk, I am. Everything in my experience has led me here to this place. When I see the little ones in the center, when I see them walking down the road, when I see them dancing at the pow-wows, I see me. I see that little girl that was me in each and every one of them. This is my reason for being here.

This is *why* I am.

Desiree

Excuse me for talking like this, but I'm so pissed off right now I'm just shaking. I just came from that school. I wanted to tell them to go f--- themselves, but I just sat there and took it, biting my lip so hard I could taste blood. Them people are always telling what's wrong with us and how we should be raising our kids and all, and I just get sick of it. You know? Sometimes I just want to punch someone just hard. If that bitch teacher says one more thing to piss me off, I'm going to.

They're telling me that my girl belongs in the special behavior class. Desiree ain't no angel, but what about all them White kids that are always raising hell? Do you see them sitting in any special classes? Shit no. And what is this assessment B.S. they keep telling me about? So someone checked this and that on a piece of paper, and that shows she belongs in that room. They ain't seen her here at home helping me with her brothers. She takes care of them like a big sister should. And they ain't seen her in the summer when she works for the rez cleanup crew and gives me some of her check so we have enough to live on. None of them A-holes were there with that f------ sheet of paper to check off that. They ain't seen her at ceremonies. They ain't seen her help her aunties. They ain't ever seen her bring food to elders at the pow-wows. They ain't ever seen her dance. She moves so strong, so beautiful, it makes me cry sometimes I'm so proud of her. They ain't ever seen her selling my crafts and giving me the money. They ain't ever seen her give the hindquarters of every deer she ever shot to those who need it more than we do.

I'm just so damn tired of hearing them always tell me what's wrong with my girl. Like she's some damn demon child or something, 'cause she ain't.

Maybe they should be assessed, put themselves in a class with behavior problems for the way they treat us Indians. For the way everyone in every f------ store we walk into follows us around like we're gonna steal something. For the way they talk to us like we are f------ deaf every time we walk into that school to hear the bad news they are always dishing out to us. For the way they pretty near put every one of our kids in those special classrooms, and say they're all gangbangers and won't amount to nothing. For all the lies they spread about us in their history books and for ignoring the real truth. For teaching Spanish and French, and now Mandarin Chinese, for Chrissakes, but then lying to the Indian parent committee that they can't afford to hire an Ojibwe language teacher because the school is broke. For the way they think all of us are nothing but lazy, good-for-nothing drunks. They should check off a sheet for all that.

If there's anyone that needs a behavior class, it's them. If there's anyone who needs to learn how to behave, it's them.

THIS ALL STARTED about a year ago. Desiree was thirteen and in the seventh grade. She told me she was going to basketball practice every day after school, but that day the school called and said she couldn't be in basketball because of her grades and the fact she'd been missing too much school. I didn't know a thing about any of that. I told them I made sure she was on the bus every morning. So when the school called that day and told me all of that I was really shook, because all along I thought things were going great for Desiree, especially when she had a tough time after her grandpa died.

"Mom, I'll catch a ride home after practice with Mel," she'd been saying every day on her way out the door. Mel's her friend, and was on the basketball team as well. Her mother had a car you could trust to make it into town and back, so she always picked her daughter up after practice.

So every weeknight Desiree was getting dropped off at home about 7:30 p.m. or so and here she wasn't even in basketball. And many times she'd come in talking about practice and here she was spinning a big tale to me and like some sucker I'd been soaking it all in like it was all the truth. I guess I had no reason not to believe her. I just know when I found out she was lying to me I had this whole rush of feelings—sad, angry, anxious . . . maybe more angry than anything. But still, she was my little girl, my Desiree. And there was love mixed in there with the anger as well. Love.

"Mrs. Strong?" It was the school woman's voice on the other end of the line. "Is this Desiree Ogema's mother?" She got that Ogema name from that worthless father of hers.

"This is she," I said in a flat tone, expecting bad news. Schools never call with good news.

"This is the school. Mrs. Strong, is Desiree home today? She's been absent quite a bit lately and it's becoming a concern."

Phone calls like that were so hard. Like getting punched right in the stomach. I didn't even know what to say at first. My lips were all dry. Then I said I would talk to her when she came home from basketball practice and that school lady told me she wasn't even in basketball, either. So then I really started worrying. Where was she? Where had she been spending her days? A lot of things start racing through your mind when things like this happen. Was she hanging around with some boyfriend? Was she using? Then of course I really started to worry about her getting hurt or killed, and I started to think about the cops pulling in the driveway and telling me something awful had happened to her. Bad news was my life. I'd had some pretty rugged times and had more than my share of bad news. Still, you never got used to it. It still hurt. You might look just hard on the outside but inside you're just lost and bawling.

So anyways, I sat there by the window waiting for her to come home that day and pretty soon it was 7:45 p.m., then 8:00 p.m. At 8:15, I called Gerri, Mel's mother, but the phone just rang on and on, no answer. Then I put my little ones, Derek and Justin, down for the night, and as I came walking down the stairs I saw headlights snaking in the driveway, and it was Desiree slamming the car door and walking down the path toward the door swinging her gym bag as she went.

Of course I was right there at the door when she walked in.

"Where you been?" I couldn't hide being pissed off. I could hardly talk I was so mad. My lower lip was just shaking.

"Holy," she said. "Geez, I been at practice. You know that."

"You ain't been at no practice," I started in on her, my voice getting higher and louder, and her spitting those lies, and then she stormed into her room and slammed the door, and I heard her saying, "I hate this f------ place."

And I was hollering at her to watch her mouth or I'd wash it out with soap, and I wanted to go in her room and just slap her. But I didn't because I had to get control of myself before this got out of control and she ended up storming out the door, and then what would I do?

Then just as quickly as it all started the house got quiet again and I had to have a smoke and I fumbled with the pack and had trouble with the lighter because my hands were shaking. Soon enough I was pacing the living room and puffing away like a freight train and trying to calm down. And then my mind was racing and wondering if I had to worry about her sneaking out her window as soon as I went to bed so she wouldn't have to face me in the morning, so I ended up sitting up half the night like some kind of watch dog.

I relived her whole life that night. My Desiree.

She was born at the Indian hospital in Cass Lake when we were living up on Leech Lake rez. Even the nurses said she was the most beautiful Indian baby you ever saw. I was only sixteen myself and still a kid. That worthless father of hers was eighteen. We were living with his parents after my dad kicked me out when he found out I was pregnant. That was a whole other story. What do you do when you're out on the street, pregnant? My mom, I remembered, she was just begging my dad to let me stay at home. I remembered she was crying and calling him every name in the book, but he was stubborn as ever, and once he stood his ground there was no changing his mind. I got that stubborn streak from him, that miserable SOB. So that's how I ended up living with Desiree's father on Tract 33, the rez housing project, up there in Cass Lake.

Desiree was a beautiful little girl, she still is. She was an easy baby. Slept all night most of the time. I tried to be a good parent, but you know when you're still a kid yourself, I just missed having fun myself and I suppose sometimes I left her with sitters I'd never leave anyone with now that I'm older, so I could go out and have a good time once in a while. But I always made sure she was clean and had decent clothes and stuff like that.

Anyway, her father disappeared when Desiree was only about six months old, and I was out on the street again because I couldn't just stay there with his parents, and I was sleeping on couches of friends with my baby and doing whatever I could to get by—cleaning their houses, babysitting, stuff like that. That went on for quite a few months, and then I finally was able to get on AFDC (Aid for Families of Dependent Children) and find my own place. I found out that worthless father of hers moved to the Cities. He hasn't shown his skinny ass around me ever since. Eventually, when Desiree was about eighteen months old, I moved back to Fond du Lac to my parents'.

I guess my dad forgave me, or whatever. Finally, when I was twenty-one, I got my own place through rez housing. Like I said, my dad, he seemed to forget and forgive. Me, I still resent his kicking me out back then when it seemed I needed help more than ever.

I had other boyfriends and ended up having two more children—boys—from one of them. That man didn't work out, either. He liked to drink and fight, and I was afraid of him because he'd get really snaky sometimes and be pushing and punching me around. Finally, I had enough of it and told my dad, and he came over and beat the shit out of him, and I never saw his fat abusive ass again, either. My boys, they're just in the third and fourth grade, so they aren't causing me any grief yet. But Desiree is fourteen, and I'm afraid my trou-bles with her might just be beginning.

DAD REALLY TOOK a shine to Desiree. When she was lit-tle, he and mom would take her on the pow-wow trail with them in summers. Mom made her a dance outfit and taught her to dance. She'd spend most of her summer weekends traveling all over Minnesota and Wisconsin with them going from pow-wow to pow-wow. She became a good dancer, really good. And they were teaching her other things as well, like to be respectful and helpful.

My dad had a stroke last year. It happened on a Friday and it was a massive one. I took Desiree in to see him on Sunday night, just before he passed. I was okay until she started crying when she seen him like that and then I let loose, too.

Us Indians, we lose so many people along the way. I lost my first brother when I was fourteen. He killed himself when he was drunk. It was winter and he'd been drunk for months and on the streets in Duluth and sleeping who knows where, not eating, mixing booze and pills and who knows what else. I couldn't even cry when my dad came and told me about him because I suppose I had been expecting that to happen sooner or later. Later that night, when I was lying there by myself, I was thinking about my brother when he was a little boy, how we used to go sledding, and how he would protect me on the school bus from all those miserable White kids. To see the little boy that he was in my memory, and then to see him drunk with all the hurt he carried. Then I cried real soft because I didn't want to wake anyone and the tears just ran down my face. Sometimes when I cry like that I just wail. There is no pain as complete, as perfect as grief. Someone said that when we cry, we lose the ability to speak. Then a year later, my baby brother died in a car accident. He wasn't driving. Didn't matter. He and two of his buddies got killed when they ran into some birch trees.

So my mom, she has had to bury two of her boys, and then my dad, and I wonder how she can even live with that pain, but she manages. I think I would not survive if I lost any of my children. I cannot even imagine that.

I think Desiree was hurt deep to the bone when my dad died. She was his favorite. I remember I went into her room and woke her up to tell her but when she saw me she already knew just by the look in my eyes.

"Pappa," she said. I still remember her crying that over and over again that night he died. She was a sixth grader then. So if there was anything I could point to that began that long spiral downward for her, I think that would probably be it.

SO AFTER THAT DAY I found out she'd been skipping school and lying about basketball and all that shit, I put her on a short leash and it seemed to work, at least for a while. I made sure she came home right after school off the bus. I called the school once a week to make sure she was there, too. And I wouldn't let her go anywhere with any of her friends unless I knew there was an adult who would keep a close eye on them.

"Hey, Mom," she'd call me sometimes when she was at her friend Mel's house, "Can I stay overnight? Me and Mel are playing video games, and it's lots of fun."

And of course, I'd melt and let her stay, but I'd make sure to have her put Gerri on the phone to make sure it was okay.

So, anyways, for a couple of months things were pretty rosy. But shit, then I guess all hell broke loose 'cause one day the phone rang and it was that school lady on the phone and she said could I come in and get Desiree 'cause she was suspended for fighting. And my f------ car wasn't running and I had to catch a ride from my mom, and then I went storming in the school and there Desiree was sitting in the principal's office acting all bad.

She got in a fight with some White girl, she said. "That bitch was calling me squaw behind my back, and nobody does that to me."

"So what about that other girl?" I said to that fat-ass principal. "She gonna get suspended, too?"

And he told me what I thought I was going to hear. "Mrs. Strong, the other girl was attacked by Desiree." Then he went on about how that White girl wasn't going to be suspended and all and I went off on him and told him a few things, and then I took Desiree and we went home.

I thought about putting her in the tribal school after that because that f------ town school was so damn racist. I had to put up with the same shit when I was there. But then I knew that tribal school had all the kids that had been pushed out of the public school, and I didn't want my girl hanging with any of those losers, either.

So when Desiree was home that five days for being kicked out of school, I had my mom take her 'cause I was working then as a substitute cook for Head Start. But I found my mom was a real pushover and was letting Desiree do whatever she felt like and feeding her sweets and watching TV all day and being on vacation more than being kicked out of school.

Well, after that she went back to school, and then it was something every week. They could have set me up with my own office there because I seemed to be spending all my time dealing with something Desiree was up to. I was trying to think of all the things.

Smoking in the girl's bathroom.

Skipping school.

Swearing at a couple of teachers.

"They're racist," she'd say. That was always her excuse, and although I knew it was true, I'd tell her that was what they wanted. They wanted to see you out of there. They were doing it just to get you riled up. But still, I got sick of her using that as an excuse all the time, too.

Getting sent out of the in-school suspension room for insubordination.

Having a shouting match with some town girls.

Sleeping in study hall.

Being late to class after class after class.

Refusing to dress for gym.

"I ain't wearing them gym clothes," she told the gym teacher. I told her she ain't got nothing to show off anyway but she wouldn't listen to me either.

Raising hell on the bus.

"Everyone raises hell on the bus," she said to me.

"We ain't talking about everyone else," I'd say, "We're talking about you."

But she would just sneer and fold her arms and sit there on the couch and clam up and pretty soon I realized it was like lecturing to the wall and she would go off in her room, and I wouldn't see her until the next day and she would come out like nothing happened.

I got to know every crack in the sidewalk leading to that school. And that school lady at the front desk of the principal's office as well, she was calling me by my first name by then.

"Renee," she'd say, looking like she was feeling sorry for my ass because I had this miserable kid. "Desiree can be such a sweet girl sometimes, but sometimes she can be such a rascal, too."

Of course, I just wanted to go tell her to go screw herself because I was so pissed off at the time, and who in the hell calls anyone "rascal" anymore, anyway?

Desiree's grades took a nosedive as well. D's in art and music. F's in social, English, gym, and math. That second quarter of the eighth grade, she was suspended eight of forty-two days, and sitting in in-school suspension seven more. That's a third of the time she wasn't even in classes, and it wasn't even counting the days she skipped school.

Now sometimes, you know, I didn't even want to talk to her 'cause I was afraid of how it would come out.

So then just a couple of weeks ago I got this letter from the school.

March 1, 2015
Ms. Renee Strong
34 Fond du Lac Homes
Cloquet, Minnesota 55720

Dear Mrs. Strong:

The Middle School Intervention Team would like to schedule a meeting with you next Thursday, March 8 at 10:00 a.m. in the school conference room to discuss Desiree. The team consists of Dave Hall (counselor), Britt Johnson (Indian homeschool social worker aide), Mary Courier (Special Education), and Josie White (Assistant Principal).

Sincerely,
Mary Courier, Team Leader

I think when I read that letter I felt like I was ready to give up because I just couldn't go into that school one more time and listen to them tell me what was wrong with Desiree, and implying all along what was wrong with me as a parent, and what was wrong with us Indians. And I guess I was just tired of hearing nothing but bad news all the time and them people being so damn condescending and acting like this was my fault.

That letter just sat on my lap, and I thought about Desiree and what was going on with her, and I couldn't help but think about what a sweet little girl she was, and all the good in her as well. 'Cause on the living room wall was a picture of my girl when she was nine years old and she was so sweet, and I remembered my mom and dad had that picture taken at Kmart on their way back from a pow-wow where Desiree had won the girl's fancy shawl category and we were all so proud of her.

"Mom," she had said when she came running into the house, her grandparents just getting out of the car to come in as well, "Mom, I won!"

She won $100 and I was so proud of her that day. She still had her hair ties on, beaded ones with the eagle fluffs. The ones I made just for her. Anyway, she gave me fifty dollars of her prize money, and said, "Mom, you need it more than me," and my eyes welled up, and I put my hands up to my lips to catch myself from bawling then and there I was so proud of my girl.

And she still showed in many ways she was a nice girl, you know. She helped clean the house and I didn't even have to push her much to help. And she knew we share washing dishes, and when I was folding clothes she'd come over and fold with me. And sometimes when she thought no one could hear, I could hear her singing in her room, and she has the voice of an angel, she does.

My little girl, Desiree, I just love her so much it makes me cry thinking what was going on with her right now.

So on that day I met with the intervention team I tried to go into that school thinking in a good way 'cause I knew it wasn't going to do no good to be otherwise and maybe I even smiled at the school lady at the reception desk who was calling me Renee, and she gave me a big smile right back. Her sitting there with a Saturday beauty salon 'do and perfect, long red manicured fingernails, and in a dress I was sure was at least a hundred bucks, and me in my baggy-ass jeans and a four-dollar Walmart blouse I bought at some rummage sale somewhere, and cheap tennies that have taken me everywhere. Her in a job I was sure she didn't even need except she'd be bored at home, and me wishing I had one.

"I'll buzz Ms. Courier to take you to the conference room," she said to me.

So I sit there in the office reception and eventually this fat bitch I ain't ever seen before came in and said she was Ms. Courier and she was leaning down talking to me like I was some kind of retard and deaf and shit, and I just wanted to blast her right there because I could tell she was going to be lecturing me because I was just some dumb reservation Indian who didn't know a thing.

Anyway, I was still trying to act nice and all, just barely, and I was sure that phony smile on my face was looking more like a snarl by then, and off we went to the conference room.

To make a long story short, they all ganged up on me and said that Desiree may have a disability, and they wanted to assess her, and if she was in need of special services, then that was just what she would receive. I was especially disappointed in Britt Johnson, the Indian Social Worker Aide, because she sat through the whole thing like she was in some kind of coma and didn't utter a peep. Now, I knew she was supposed to be the advocate for us Indians, and here she was selling out to them. Them Johnsons were nothing but a bunch of hang-around-the-fort Indians anyway.

But I was on my best behavior, even if that Courier bitch was irritating the hell out of me with her condescending yak yak yak about Desiree this, and we were only concerned about Desiree and all that phony B.S.

So I left there that day pretty pissed off but proud of myself because I didn't rank off on anyone and I signed that paper saying they could assess my girl.

About a week later I got another letter and they scheduled a meeting with the team and the school psychologist and that's when they told me that she belonged in the special class for kids with behavior disorders. And that fatass Courier bitch teacher, I just wanted to punch her, she was sitting there so damn righteous when the psychologist was telling me what was going on with Desiree and how this was the right thing and all, and me just wanting to crawl into a hole somewhere I was feeling so low.

THAT NIGHT ME and the kids went over to Mom's and I asked her if she would watch my boys because I wanted to take Desiree to see Lester Northbird. He did healing. I had called him as soon as I got back from that school conference, and he said I could come on over and he had the time to see Desiree. He said to bring a new blanket, tobacco, and anything I could offer, and he would work on her.

I been to see him myself before. Like when my dad died I was in such pain, maybe more for my mom and Desiree than myself, but I needed some healing on the inside, and going to see Lester helped a lot because he prayed over me for a long time, and when I told him about all my pain he spoke about that pain to the spirits who took it up to the Creator to pity me, and help me cope and all.

I had Desiree hand Lester the blanket and sacred *asema* and she was just shy and that little girl again and not the angry one I saw so much now. And he took her in the back room where he does his doctoring and when they came out I thanked him and slipped him twenty dollars—all I had—and I knew it was worth it 'cause sometimes we needed a spiritual intervention when things got really rugged and nothing else helped.

Those White people knew nothing about assessment. Lester, he could just look right into your soul and tell what was wrong. He could see right through all the pain we carried, all the hurt, and he could take it and ask the spirits to help us make sure our Creator had pity on us, and take it from us and cast it into the wind.

Lester the assessor. Hey, that rhymed.

That night after we picked up the boys and got home, I asked Desiree if she would stay up for a while and we went into the living room and I asked her if she'd like some tea.

"Mom," she said, and she was surprised because I'd never offered her tea before. That was something we usually only did with adults when they were visiting.

"Come here, my girl," I said, and my voice was cracking, although I was trying to hide it, but she could tell I was really holding back a good bawling.

"I wish your pappa were here right now," I continued, and I was crying by then. And then she was sitting right by me and holding my hand, and her head was rested on my shoulder like she would do when she was just a little girl and the world was closing in on her and she needed me just then.

And we talked.

We talked almost the half the night. I told her everything about when I was fifteen, just a year older than she was then, and how I ended up pregnant and how her grandfather kicked me out, and of trying to survive on nothing. I told her about when she was born and how the nurses at the Cass Lake Indian Hospital said she was the most beautiful Indian baby they ever seen. And I told her about her real father, even though he was worthless, and I tried to think of good things to say even though I had to make some things up and twist the story to make him look a little like a good guy and all. And I told her about the boys' father. Then I told her about that life journey we were all on, and how my journey had sometimes been a pretty rugged one and that I didn't want to see her stumble the way I had. That I didn't want to see her pregnant so young like me. That I wanted her to get the education I never was able to get and wanted to see her graduate and go on and make something of herself and go back to that school and show them.

She cried all through this story I told her. Then when it was over we lightened up, and we laughed together for the first time in a long, long time.

And she says, "Mom, I'll try. I'll try to do better. I will. I'll try. I love you, Mom."

My Desiree. I love her so.

When I looked in her eyes, I saw the mirror of myself.

See, them school people, they only see one side of her. They ain't seen her here at home helping me with her brothers. She takes care of them like a big sister should. And they ain't seen her in the summer when she works for the rez cleanup crew and gives me some of her check so we have enough to live on. None of them A-holes were there with that f------ sheet of paper to check off that. They ain't seen her at ceremonies. They ain't seen her help her aunties. They ain't ever seen her bring food to elders at the pow-wows. They ain't ever seen her dance. She moves so strong, so beautiful, it makes me cry sometimes I'm so proud of her. They ain't ever seen her selling my crafts and giving me the money. They ain't ever seen her give the hindquarters of every deer she ever shot to those who need it more than we do.

That school. They look at our kids and right off they start checking off all the things wrong with them. They never see the other side, the parts we see. They don't even know it exists.

Maybe someone needs to come up with a way of assessing the whole child. Then they would know my Desiree. Then maybe they could say things and I would listen.

A Wolf Story
Part One:
The Arrival

A fictional story of the arrival of French fur traders to the Ojibwe settlement on Madeline Island, Wisconsin, on the south shore of Lake Superior, approximately 1644, as told by the spirit of a wolf.

~*Thomas D. Peacock*

My earth is the moon over the lake, the vapor of our breaths when we run hard through fields on cold fall nights with the stars all above and around us and shining off the perfect calm of the water. My earth is tracking deer on cold winter days, the chase and precise timing of the kill, and then of sleeping curled together for warmth in deep snow, our mouths covered in fresh, dried blood from our feasting. My earth is of the dark and wind and perfect stillness before a summer storm and the sounds of slow, rolling thunder off the lake, echoing through the trees. My earth is the smell of wet grass and wildflowers, and all the bright colors of the land and water and sky.

We have lived the entirety of our lives on this sacred island, the place we know as Turtle Island, the island of islands, on this lake, I along with *Waubun Anung* (Dawn Star), my mate, and all of our relatives—brothers and

154

sisters, cousins, aunties and uncles, nephews and nieces. There are scarcely fifteen of us, but we are all family with one beginning, one grandmother, all of us together.

It was late in the season of falling leaves, and we had been tracking a mother deer and her two young ones near the western shore when we saw the new man-wolves coming across the water from the mainland in vessels made from the meat and outer skin of trees, toward us, toward our island. And although I rarely knew fear, there was something about the sight of them that raised the hairs on the back of my neck, but I tried not to show it because I would never let the others know that I possessed fear. We had discerned their scent long before they were sighted, and it contained smells we didn't recognize and found confusing. For sure, there were familiar smells of fire and ashes, sweat, piss, and bear grease, but there were other things we did not recognize that were new to us and not of the islands, nor to Turtle Island, the island of islands. Even their muffled voices in the distance sounded strange and new and made us wonder. And once they were close enough for us to discern their language, we were certain right away these were a whole new kind of man-wolves because it took us some time before we were able to translate their new tongue to our thoughts. As they came near shore, we crouched hidden behind great white pines and saw they were very pale in complexion, almost like the clouds on cold, fall days, and there were several among them who seemed to have no color whatsoever in their eyes, and most had fur grown all on their faces, and the hair on their heads were many shades of light and dark. Nor did we recognize the animal skins they wore to cover their nakedness, and maybe their garments weren't from animals at all, for they were new to us. But mostly it was their scent, overwhelming, and we sensed coming away these were creatures whose bodies never knew the sweat lodge, or the cleansing waters of the lake, or fresh cedar boughs.

I counted seven of them, all males.

Ogema (leader), a voice entered my thoughts, calling to me. We should have killed them just as they were stepping ashore, as soon as the clunking of their canoes touched the first rocks of the shoreline, as soon as their moccasins touched the rich earth of our homeland. Maybe I should have heeded the thoughts of my cousin, *Andig* (Crow), the black one, who had once challenged me to be leader, who still hated me deep in the recesses of his heart, who had once felt my fury, who may have smelled the scent of my fear at their coming, who had early on sent the thought out to all of us: Kill them. Kill them now before it is too late. Instead we lay hidden and watching until the sun moved late across the sky as the newcomers set up camp, built fire, cooked and ate a meal.

We lay there watching them for a long time, in perfect silence, practiced since we were pups, learned well. Later, as we finally left our watching place and returned to the north end of the island, I asked one of my nephews to stay and to report back to us of their doings. And when we returned to our village we gathered in circle and talked about the new man-wolves, of their coming and strong scent and unfamiliar tongue and of the fur on their faces, the strange skins covering their nakedness, and skin the color of death, and eyes and hair of many shades of light and dark. We should kill them, *Andig* repeated to us. You are showing weakness not to do this, he said to me. To hesitate is to foreshadow our demise. You have always been weak that way. There is no good in these new wolves.

These are not our brothers.

But I reminded him and the others that we were intimately connected to the man-wolves. That even these strange new ones were our brothers as well, just as the old man-wolves with whom we shared the island were our relatives, that all wolves shared a common story. And I tried to assure them, convince them, especially the older warriors among us, and *Waubun Anung* pulled the she-wolves aside, her sister and cousins and aunties, and did the same. We all share a common story, we repeated. These are our brothers.

And later in the evening when the nephew returned he told us what he had learned of their ways, and of why they had come, and we wondered more what their coming meant to us, for us.

And as we lay sleepless, wondering, Old Uncle, my father's brother, gathered us all together in story, an old, familiar story, often told, practiced:

After all of the earth and sky were made, the Creator instructed first man to travel to all the corners of the earth and give names to all the plants, animals, and places of the Creation. And he did as he was instructed, naming everything, the day and night and seasons, and the circle of all things. Nothing was left untouched by his travels.

Yet he walked alone and noticed that all other animals walked in pairs. And he was lonely and said to his Creator, "I am alone." And the Creator sent someone to walk with him, and that was Ma-en'gun *(Wolf), our grandfather, the grandfather of all wolves.*

Man and Wolf walked all the corners of the earth and became very close, as brothers. When this was done, the Creator called them to him again and told them they must now part ways—man one way, wolf the other.

"From this day on, you are to separate your paths. You must go your different ways.

"What shall happen to one of you will also happen to the other. Each of you will be feared, respected and misunderstood by the people that will later join you on this earth."

Then Old Uncle reminded us that the Creator gave us the land and waters where we lived in honor of the brotherhood of wolf and man, that *Gitche Gummi* (Lake Superior) bore the likeness of a wolf's head as a reminder of our place and purpose there.

This is the teaching, he said, and it is so.

So in the early morning stillness when we finally gathered to sleep in close circle around Old Uncle to keep his tired bones warm, we dreamed of the story and of our place here on the earth, and our relationship to first man, and to his descendants.

Those we call the man-wolves.

WE ARE AN ANCIENT TRIBE. My ancestors have been a part of the land nearly since the creation of the four-leggeds, and have lived here in the great forests along the shores of the lake for over 10,000 winters, following the great herd animals here with the retreat of the last glacier. In that early time, they seldom hungered for food, because the land provided a garden of elk and caribou and buffalo and deer upon which to feast. And closely following my ancestors to the area have been different waves of man-wolves, also in pursuit of the herds—man-wolves whose names have long been forgotten, who migrated on to other places, or disappeared, or intermarried with other tribes. Each of the various waves of man-wolves would, on occasion, steal one of our pups and raise it to pull their belongings, or use it to befriend their children and elders, or keep it to curl next to them in the deep of winter for warmth. They even gave the pups a new name, *animush* (dog). Often the dogs would be trained to hunt or protect their villages because of their vastly superior sense of smell and sight, because what remains wolf in them are the ability to be keen listeners, watchers. These dogs, of course, would eventually become more like man-wolves themselves, and forget many of the wolf ways we have perfected to ensure our survival all of these eons. Now, dogs seem nearly useless to us, only useful to the man-wolves.

There are the more recent man-wolves that call themselves *Dakotah* and *Meshkwahkihaki* (Fox). Then about 150 winters ago came the *Anishinaabeg* Ojibwe, settling in great numbers along the shores of the lake and these sacred islands. They established their first village on our island home, and called it *Moningwanakuning* (Madeline Island), the place of the yellow-breasted woodpecker, the place we know as Turtle Island. The place they also refer to as the turtle-shaped island of their prophecies.

When the Ojibwe first arrived here we were very curious, as that is our nature, and we crept close enough to their villages to listen, in the dark, deep trees to watch, and learn their stories and ways. We learn a lot in our watching and listening, in the perfect silence that is broken only by the muffled voices of the storytellers. In this way we learned many things about these new creatures. We, of course, have our own stories, and have always known and passed them down, including the story of creation now told by Old Uncle. So it was to our utter amazement early in their first winter when they gathered in their wigwams, the Ojibwe told their stories, and among the stories was the one of first man and *Ma-en'gun*, our grandfather, the grandfather of all wolves. And we knew at once, of course, that these were the people of our prophecies, that these were the descendants of original man, and that we share a common story, that they came to the lake and to this sacred island, Turtle Island, the island of islands, to live out the story.

And now new man-wolves had arrived. Nephew, who I had posted to watch and listen to the newcomers, told us these were *adawe winineeg* (traders), who had come to trade their wares with the Ojibwe for the furs of the beaver, fox, ermine, otter, and other animal relatives. And he told us that they carried magic sticks that breathed fire, and that the fire was a killing weapon, more powerful than any club, or bow, or spear, or teeth, and that it ran faster than any creature could run. That he had seen them take down a deer with the fire, and that the animal at once fell dead. That it did not try to rise and run from death. That it did not cry out. That it did not thrash about on the ground in its final struggle. And that made us wonder of the fate of our relatives, and ultimately, of us.

They had scarcely been on the island for more than several days when they went among the Ojibwe and offered them gifts—samples of the wares we had never seen before or knew their purposes, wares used to take down trees, skin both animals and plants, as well vessels for cooking over the fire because their soft teeth and weak stomachs had forgotten the beauty of raw meat, beautifully woven skins made from animals or plants foreign to us which they used to cover their nakedness, and tiny stones of many colors which they used to decorate the skins, as well to wear as decoration. Late one night as they slept I had Nephew steal into their camp and take one of the woven skins and bring it back to our village, where we all wondered about its softness, took turns rolling in it to leave our scent, and when we grew bored of it left to the pups to fight over. They eventually tore it to shreds, as pups sometimes do, and scattered it all over the ground.

Over the cycle of a moon we watched in the distance as the new man-wolves established themselves on the island. And we observed how the newcomers and Ojibwe so quickly became confidants, that several of the new ones even courted the Ojibwe females, taking them back to their dens where they exchanged the common language of lovemaking. The males of the two tribes began exchanging material things and foodstuffs—the beautiful small stones for maple sugar cakes, colorful strips of the material used to cover their nakedness for some of the cache of wild rice, a cooking vessel for the hides of deer, or several pairs of moccasins.

Spokesmen would sit in council with each other most every day. We are willing, they said, to trade the things we possess for the furs of certain animals, and we will give you, in advance, a weapon to lure these creatures and ensnare them so they cannot run away. And at first the Ojibwe were leery of the prospects of this trade because their teachings spoke strongly to them that all things of *aki* (mother earth) are related, that the animal and plant beings are their elder brothers, that to claim the meat of another creature should only be done for sustenance, to survive, and that there are certain songs and prayers that are said when this is done to ensure the spirit of the creature is respected, that all of this is done in humility. And they knew as well, because the stories were told in every winter around their lodges, that their prophecies warned of a time when they would be tempted by the desire for material possessions. And their elders reminded them of these things each day after the new man-wolves left their village.

We know, however, that man-wolves are not perfect beings, and that they often stray from the Good Path, *mino-bimaadiziwin*; that although in each of them are these beautiful and gentle ways, that the very essence of the Creator that was given to all creatures at their conception also has an opposite. That in each and every man-wolf is an inherent struggle. That influencing them in the external world dwells an Other.

So among the Ojibwe, the debates went on for days about whether to accept the snares of the new man-wolves. And always the Other spoke in the ears of the Ojibwe in a strong voice for its desire to possess the new wares—of vessels made of a shiny stone that were superior to the bark vessels they cooked in, of skins softer and warmer than the hides used to cover them, of cutting tools made of the shiny stone, and even the possibility of possessing the sticks that breathed fire, which they knew at once were vastly superior to the club, spear, or bow, and which could be used to quickly overpower their enemies. The debate went on in the circle of the fire as well within each individual.

And as we watched and listened from the distance we were reminded of the beauty of their sweat lodge, how the individual leading the sweat would always acknowledge the presence of the Other and its power, and ask it to leave the proceedings, for just a while, so the prayers and healings and discussions of the sweat could be pure.

This time, however, the request was not made, and the Other spoke strongly, certainly more strongly than the voices of reason, and in the end the Ojibwe accepted the new man-wolves' snares. And when their council made its decision we heard the spirits of all the animals cry out in the wind.

As soon as the spirit of winter won in its struggle against the spirit of fall and snow fell over the island, we began witnessing the results of the decision. And we observed how certain animals were lured into the snares and trapped, and how they suffered in their struggle to free themselves, and how they died without dignity, without the proper songs and prayers being said. Mostly, however, we saw that when their furs were gathered how their carcasses were sometimes carelessly left on the ground for the cleaners—the crows and ravens, gulls, mice, flies, worms. The manner of these deaths disrespected everyone and everything involved, and overshadowing the grisly ritual was a kind of greed, a shadow so dark that light would not cleave.

And then came the day when *Waubun Anung*, my mate, along with Old Uncle, took several of the younger ones to the west side of the island in hopes of gathering rabbits and several other small animals for a feast. I know now the moment of the happening because I am certain I heard the singing of spirit voices, *Waubun Anung's* grandmother, mother, and old aunties, as well the pups she bore that did not survive birth, all of them singing. And when I heard this, I ran toward where they had gone, and was met by several of my nieces, running at full gate, weeping. And I cried out her name, and her spirit answered me.

I looked in vain for her as well Old Uncle and one of the young ones. And then after what seemed like the longest time I was joined by *Andig*, the black one, and one of the other warriors. We are here to help find our sister, uncle, and niece, he sent his thoughts to me. I could not hide my fear and rage for what fate had become of the three missing ones, and *Andig* came to me and assured me, because in times like that we are family and any animosities we may have had for each other are inconsequential.

In time we found them. From what it appeared, *Waubun Anung* had been ensnared by one of the traps and Old Uncle and one of our nieces had stayed on with her to help free her, comfort her. The new man-wolves, however, must have heard their cries of distress and found them there. They were slaughtered in that place, their hides having been removed, leaving only their carcasses. I was wild with grief and rage and *Andig* and the other warrior had to calm me, console me. Not now, *Ogema*, he sent his thoughts to me. Now is not a good time for atonement. Now is the time to grieve and pray and send our relatives on their westward journey to the land of souls. Now is not the time for atonement. That will come later.

So while the other two began the ritual of prayers and songs of grieving over Old Uncle, my mate, and our niece, I made my way up the length of the island to a sacred place on the northwestern shore, to an outcropping overlooking the lake where through the great pines there was a clear view of many of the other islands—the island of small bears, the island of visions, the island of red berries, the island of great hills, the island of spirits, the island of eagles, and the island of caves—a place my mate and I had often come when we were young and new to love, and that we would also come as adults as a reminder of our commitment to one another.

And I grieved there for four days as is our custom, repeating all the prayers and songs and singing a traveling song. Although reason told me her spirit was making its westward journey to the land of souls to be with all of our relatives who had walked on and that she would be happy there with our Creator, where she would no longer suffer —never again feel hunger or cold or pain—the reality of her loss weighed heavily on me.

For in my pain, it seemed that all promise died with her.

And on the evening of the fourth day, she visited me in my dreams and told me she had arrived home safely, and that her grandmother and mother and old aunties, and all the pups she bore that did not survive birth met her on the other side of the river, and that they led her to the great village of our Creator, and that I need not grieve or wonder anymore of her suffering. And when I awoke in the darkness of early morning the sky was filled with stars and the Milky Way lay wrapped across the whole of the sky like a warm blanket, and the morning star of her namesake shone in all its brightness down on me.

A PLAN OF ATONEMENT was set in motion as soon as I returned to our village. At first, Nephew was sent to watch and listen near the Ojibwe settlement and when it was time he signaled our warriors, who went into the heart of the old man-wolves' settlement in the dark of night and stole away with the several dogs they kept so they would not warn their masters of our presence. And then just several nights later, *Andig* and the other warriors raided the Ojibwe's food cache of just enough of their winter reserves so they would only have enough to make it through winter. And we did this out of love for them, our brothers. Brothers who had forgotten the reasons they had come to the island, the place we call Turtle Island, the island of islands. The place they knew as the turtle-shaped island of their prophecies. Brothers who had heeded to the demands of the Other, who had somehow been blinded by their desire for things, who had forgotten their relationship and responsibility to their relatives, the animal and plant beings, brothers who had forgotten the teachings of their prophets. Brothers who had forgotten the story of first man and *Ma-en'gun*, our grandfather, the grandfather of all wolves, who had forgotten that their purpose in coming to this place was to live out the story.

We waited more days and then came the heavy snows, and then more snows, and finally the deep cold of winter. And then we knew it was time, and we entered the new man-wolves' encampment under the cover of darkness and quietly stole away with their entire store of food reserves, knowing that their Ojibwe neighbors would be in no position to offer any of their own reserves to the newcomers, knowing that without food the new man-wolves would never survive the winter.

We are a patient tribe. We have been here for over 10,000 winters and have observed the different waves of man-wolves and their comings and goings.

When the new man-wolves died from cold and hunger we went into the silence of their encampment. And in the warmth of spring we were there again to roll in their rotting flesh.

I was given the great honor of being the first to do so.

MY TRIBE WILL FOREVER be in this land, on this island, for our spirits run heavy in this place. We are made of the very earth of this place, Turtle Island, the island of islands.

And my spirit is the moon over the lake, the vapor of the breaths of my descendants when they run hard through fields on cold fall nights with the stars all above and around them and shining off the perfect calm of the water. My spirit is in them when they are tracking deer on cold winter days, the chase and precise timing of the kill, and then sleeping curled together for warmth in deep snow, their mouths covered in fresh, dried blood from their feasting. My spirit is of the dark and wind and perfect still-ness before a summer storm and the sounds of slow, rolling thunder off the lake, echoing through the trees. My spirit is the smell of wet grass and wildflowers, and all the bright colors of the land and water and sky.

Someday when you are out walking in the woods and you see a wolf out of the corner of your eye.

And you look that way and there is nothing there.

A Wolf Story
Part Two:
The Boy

In the year 1850, I traveled with my parents by canoe from the village of Red Cliff in what is now northwestern Wisconsin to Sandy Lake (in central Minnesota) late in the fall, where we Ojibwe were to be issued our annuity payments and rations. I was only ten years old at the time but the journey and its aftermath are forever seared in my memory. Thousands of Ojibwe from all over had gathered there. Only later, as an adult, was I to find out that government officials had lured us all there to get Wisconsin and Michigan Ojibwe to move to northwestern Minnesota. The rations and annuity payments didn't arrive as promised, and we waited until early December, when it was too late. An early winter storm hit, and then the cold weather set in. Exposure, starvation, and disease claimed the death of 170 souls there at Sandy Lake. And our canoes became worthless for travel as the lakes and rivers began to freeze, so we began the long walk home. Two hundred seventy more Ojibwe, including my parents, perished trying to reach their villages. I was one of those who were rescued, who lived. This is the story of my rescue. Mostly, however, this is the story of Ogema, my rescuer.
~Michael Bear (Miskwabekong Ojibwe)

I was born three winters ago in a litter of four, a sister, two brothers, and myself. My mother was a village dog, and I say that not meaning any disrespect in the least because she really wasn't "owned," as people call it, by any one family. We lived with and back and forth among several families in the Ojibwe village of *Miskwabekong* (the place of the red cliffs) in what is now northwestern Wisconsin along the south shore of Lake Superior, with a set of grandparents and several of their families. When we were old enough to remember, we would be told we were born under the porch of the government agent's house, which was almost halfway between the multiple residences of our owners. Don't ask me how my mother ended up having us there. If it were important, there would probably be a story that went along with it.

While my brothers and sister inherited their mother's side, the dog, I entered the world with many of the physical and behavioral traits of my father, so much so the villagers who did not know me by name often called me "wolf dog," and that made perfect sense since I am, indeed, a wolf hybrid, the product of a domestic mixed-breed mother and captive wolf father. It seems, however, that I inherited just enough from each—enough dog to be beholden to my Ojibwe human alpha, enough wolf to retain a certain wild, quiet resistance, a yearning to be free.

Wolf dog, the villagers who didn't know me by name would say to me, even when I was a young pup, and if I could have spoken in their language I would have told them my story, because I know it. Dogs, few of them know their story. Their story becomes lost in the story of their human owners. I am this person's dog, one says. I am that person's dog, another says. None of that speaks to the dog's own story. Wolves, we all know our story. Here is mine.

My *'way ay* (namer), the young Ojibwe boy who raised me, who would eventually become my alpha, named me *Ogema*, without even knowing the name was part of my ancestry. Maybe he saw something in me as a young pup. Maybe because I was bigger and stronger than my brothers or sister, maybe because I had my way with my mother's milk before they did, maybe because I comfortably took on the look and demeanor of my father, the wolf. My father, the wolf who seemed to live fluidly between the village and surrounding forests, who was never quite comfortable being owned by anyone, who was sometimes seen in the company of his wolf relatives, who preferred to live a solitary life, who did not bark, who did not wag his tail, who did not run happily to greet his human owners, who rarely spoke. Who was a watcher, a keen observer to all the subtleties and deeper meanings of things.

Who, when he did speak, told our story going back over many thousands of generations: That my line is of the wolves of Turtle Island, the island of islands, the place known to the Ojibwe as *Moningwanakaning* (the place of the yellow-breasted woodpecker), the sacred place, the place of secrets. You are a descendent of the great wolf, *Ogema*, your namesake, he said, who led a rebellion of wolves with the arrival of the first French traders, the new man-wolves as they were called then, to the island. The traders, and soon the Ojibwe, began the wholesale slaughter of the animals for their furs until they were almost completely gone, until there was only silence, until the forest wept. You are the descendant of the she-wolf, *Waubun Anung*, alpha mate of *Ogema*, who was the first wolf slaughtered by the new man-wolves. You are the descendant of a long line of wolves who have been in this place of water and islands for over ten thousand years, who followed the great herd animals to this place with the retreat of the last glacier. And he told me as well the story of our creation, of when first man and wolf walked together as brothers over the face of the earth and named all of the waters and islands and hills, the plants and animal beings, and that was *Ma-en'gun*, our grandfather, the grandfather of all wolves. That through prophesy, human and wolf share a common destiny. That the Creator gave us the land and waters of our dwelling in honor of the brotherhood of wolf and man, that *Gitche Gummi* bears the likeness of a wolf's head as a reminder of our place and purpose here. That there is a reason we live near and among the humans.

This is the teaching, he said, and it is so. Wolves, he said, we have a story.

So obviously while I am half dog, I identify most with the wolf in me, and it's not that I deny my dog side. I deeply care for my multiple human owners, especially the elderly grandparents and the boy, and having that faith and loyalty in one's human owners is definitely part of my dog side. That sense extends out to the greater village as well, because all of us "pets," as we are sometimes referred, whether we are dog or wolf, care for the wellbeing of our owners. And like many of us "pets," what we sense in our Ojibwe owners is that they are going through a difficult and troubling time, that they are experiencing a period of great uncertainty and transition in the community, and that it is not just one thing that would explain why they seem out of balance, because the troubles the Ojibwe are having just seem to be multiplying and feeding on one another all at the same time. Mostly what I sense is almost a frenzy of despair, of grieving, of a village under siege with itself. And I sense the reasons for this can all be tied to the coming of the Europeans, the humans my wolf ancestors referred to as the new man-wolves. And while it may be unfair to link all of their troubles to one thing, in this case it seems to be true.

While once the forests and lakes had forever provided for us, now there is not enough meat, not enough deer or rabbit, or even mice to harvest for nourishment. The circle of the hunts has grown much larger. Humans and wolves must work twice as hard for a single kill, if they are so fortunate. The animals whose furs were most prized by the French, and later the Americans, are scarce, so the balance of things has tipped. My wolf relatives, who once harvested the animals prized for their furs, are suffering. And at the same time the new settler's government has confined the Ojibwe into small areas upon which they are to live and make a livelihood, on bog and wetland or clay and rock with weak soils that doesn't sufficiently support their gardens. On land far removed from the wild rice lakes, which has been their primary source of food. They are quickly trading their hide and bark round lodges for the square, wooden homes of the settlers, their hide clothing for cloth, their moccasins for boots made from the hides of cattle. And now, especially in this village more so than others, it seems they have even traded the manner in which they worship the Creator, as the people have divided themselves into camps of those who worship the old way and those who have adopted the way of the settlers. And each says theirs is the only way and insists the other is wrong, and this has divided families and the community in a way it has never been before, an intolerance so far removed, so opposite and contradictory from the love and grace exemplified by the same Creator in whom they both worship.

And now the Ojibwe, who over the course of the fur trade had grown dependent on the wares of the new arrivals, who were lured by the desire to possess things—the vessels for cooking, blankets, clothing, mirrors, furniture, metal stoves, money, guns, and, now, alcohol (which in itself has made those who drink it act completely *gewanadizi*—crazy) are now also dependent upon the government of the settlers for food rations. For when the forest was emptied of the prize furbearing animals, they could no longer supply the traders with furs, and their access to the things the settlers possessed dried up. Now they are trading for the land, the earth itself, and it is not an equal trading relationship between the two because the government of the settlers knows that without food rations the Ojibwe will perish from starvation. So it seems, at least from my perspective, that a once mighty nation has been humbled and is crumbling before my very eyes. And we "pets," as we are referred to, can only watch in silence because we know that what happens to them will also beget us. That is the teaching.

For several winters, the Ojibwe had gathered by the thousands from all of their scattered villages on Turtle Island, the island of islands, to collect the annuities (small amounts of money) and food rations from the government of the settlers that they had exchanged for the land. For land now quickly being peopled by families of settlers, the good land with rich soil for growing their crops, the good land bordering rivers and lakes upon which they can easily travel by boat and canoe. The land upon which they have brought their cattle and sheep, the land upon which they are now killing wolves because my wolf relatives see the cattle and sheep as food to be harvested.

Now, the government of the settlers had told the Ojibwe that the annual settling of annuities was to be moved to a place many days west, that if they are to receive the food they needed to survive the coming winter they would have to travel there to get it. And in the village, many of the adults and their children were readying for travel, and decisions were being made regarding who would go and who would stay, provisions were being gathered—dried meat, corn, wild rice—and plans made on the route of the journey, and who would travel with who, and how long they would be gone. So in the extended family of our multiple owners, it was decided that the two younger families would do the westward journey, leaving the grandparents. And among those making the journey were the parents and little boy who is my *'way ay*, who owns me, who is no more than ten winters in human age, who I have spent nearly every day the entirety of my three years on the earth in the company of, and whose life I am sworn to protect.

So I watched as they readied for the journey, and I spent all of my waking time with the boy because I wanted to make the journey with him, and feared that if I left his side he would leave without me.

Take me with, I said, speaking through my eyes to him. My keen sense of smell and hearing and sight will be useful to you and the family as you journey. My speed and endurance and teeth will protect you from any enemies. I will curl next to you in the cold evenings for warmth. And if I could have spoken in his language, my pleading would have shouted it out. Take me with you.

On the day of their leaving, however, the boy came to me as I lay in front of the family lodge. You stay here, he said to me. You stay right here and protect our elders. They need you here to protect them from our enemies. They need you to keep them company and offer warmth in the cold evenings. And in my heart I protested because I wanted to be with him, to protect him, and he must have sensed it. No, he said. You stay here. And to emphasize the certainty of his order, he used his open hand to push me away, and I was left stunned and disappointed and angry.

Then as the people gathered and the travelers began leaving in their canoes I ran to be with him, to be by his side, and he was forced to run me off many times, and finally resorted to using a stick to drive me away, even knowing in his heart it was not right. Go home, he said. I hate you, dog, he repeated over and over again. I do not want you with. You stay here. And finally, heartbroken, believing for just that moment what he was saying was true, I finally relented, and defeated, walked slowly back to the family lodge with my head down. I hate you, he had said. I do not want you, was all I could think of.

From then on I spent most days lying in wait in the front of the lodge. And the grandparents, whom I was left to protect, waited with me, as I lay at their feet and they scratched and stroked my ears and neck and face, and scratched my belly to comfort me, and I snuggled in close to them to keep them warm and let them know that I was there to be their protector.

Ogema, they said to comfort me, the boy meant no harm in chasing you off. You have no place in their journey. You have not traded the land for food. You have no need for the settler's money. Your place is here with us.

But at night when I lay alone in front of the flap of the opening of the lodge, I dreamed of the boy and his parents, and wondered of their journey, and worried for them. And waited.

THEY HAD BEEN GONE for many evenings. And one day a young runner, a stranger, came into the village, scared and tired and hungry and out of breath. And you could see even though he was strong and had a strong voice that he was deeply troubled by what he was about to tell us, and his voice was breaking as he spoke. I am from a western village, he began, as he followed the proper protocol of telling us about his family, and clan, even though he hungered and was in need of rest, and had come to deliver somber news.

Your families are in danger, he said to those of us who had remained there in the village. The rations did not come. Then came the snow and cold. And now your people are making their journey home on foot, but there are many among them who are suffering from hunger and disease and cold. Already many have perished. They sent me here to tell you to come to them, to bring whatever food you have, to help to bury the dead.

And I was with the grandfather when I first heard the news and we quickly returned to the lodge to tell the grandmother, and then we gathered as a village in its center and the people talked about what they must do. Only a few strong men and women had been left to care for those who had stayed, and there were those who were very young or elderly, or infirmed, or those who could not travel because of injury. Who will go, they all asked, and all said they would. And they argued about it for a long time, and all the while we "pets," as they refer to us, had already made decisions about who among them should be making the journey of rescue. Because we have that sense about who was strong enough to make such journeys, because we know full well this was not the time to waste debating who will not go or go.

And the boy who I loved, who had raised me from a pup, who had named me, was all I could think about.

The village finally decided that a few strong men and boys would go, as time was of essence and there were not enough provisions for a larger party to make the journey. Where are our people, they asked the stranger, where will we find them? The reply came that the last he was aware, many were on the western end of the big lake, Lake Superior, and they were camped out waiting for warmer weather to melt some of the snow, trying to hunt for food, and tending to the sick. They will not be able to make their return without assistance, he said. They will surely perish there if no help comes to them.

As those who were selected for the journey hastily made their preparations, I made my way to the far side of the village to where my father, the wolf, lived with the boy's father's old uncle. I found him there sunning, the old man scratching his ears.

Father, I sent my thoughts to him, the boy. I was so distraught I was tripping over my words. The boy needs our help. And then I asked him to do the journey with me to find the boy and his family, to make the rescue, to keep them warm, to protect them from enemies, to assure their safe return.

He was, however, not easily swayed by my plea for help. Maybe, he said, it is not our place to interfere in the course of things, in the playing out of the people's story. Maybe this is the way things should be, maybe if we alter the way of things we will only delay the people's demise, and they will only suffer more, and longer, for many more generations. Maybe it is the Creator's wish to call them to Him so they will suffer no longer.

Father, the boy, I said. He is just a boy. He had no say in the decisions to slaughter the fur-bearing animals so the people could possess things, no say in the decisions to trade the land for food, no say in deciding whose manner of worshipping the Creator is right or wrong. He is just a boy, and I am sworn to protect him, my *'way ay*. And it is not our place to wonder what will become of the people in the future. We can only live for now, for what is happening now. And what we have in front of us now is a little boy and his family, and other families, who will surely perish without our help. That is all that should concern us now. Father, please.

And my father, the wolf, who seemed to live fluidly between the village and surrounding forests, who was never quite comfortable being owned by anyone, who was sometimes seen in the company of his wolf relatives, who preferred to live a solitary life, who did not bark, who did not wag his tail, who did not run happily to greet his human owners, who rarely spoke, who was a watcher, a keen observer to all the subtleties and deeper meanings of things, said he would help me get the boy and his family.

And with that decision began our journey to rescue them.

FATHER, WHEN WILL WE set out?

Now, he said.

We knew this would be a difficult journey for us, a journey over several days into strange territory. There would be constant danger of attack from other wolves whose territories we would infringe upon along the way, of the possibility of hunger given the scarcity of other animals from which to harvest, of the snow we would encounter, of cold. And we also knew we would have to travel without the humans, the men and boys from our village who were also making the journey on foot, because they would only hold us up. For wolves are much faster. Our eyes and nose and ears are much keener.

So we set out. We will follow the hills along the lake, said my father, always keeping the lake within view. And we will travel in the night, stopping only to rest and gather whatever food we can for energy. We will not challenge other wolves that may confront us. And if confronted, we will request permission for safe travel through their territory.

Then, traveling westward we went, running, running. At first light we stopped for water and were able to catch a vole and mice. Then to sleep, too tired to dream. Then awakening to wait, to wait more, then at dusk just when we were about to lose patience we set out again. Running, running. Then again at first light we rested again. The ground now had a dusting of snow. Again, hunting for whatever we could capture, this time we were rewarded with a salamander, hiding deep in a rotting tree stump. Then to sleep, again too tired to dream.

On the third night we heard other wolves calling in the distance. Quiet, my father said to me. We stopped for a moment, than ran a wide arc to avoid them where we could hear the voices. Running in silence, broken only by our hard breathing, the vapor from our breath trailing from our nostrils, from the hot dampness of our fur. Running, running. Then it was dawn again. Now the snow was up to our ankles. We knew, however, that was when the mice sometimes are careless, thinking that if they cannot be seen that they will somehow be safe. We, however, can hear through the snow. We feasted on mice that day. We ate snow. Sleep, a ragged dream. The boy. I saw him suffering.

On the fourth night we came upon an encampment hidden deep among a grove of cedar and hemlock. We approached cautiously, alert. Quietly, my father warned, speaking to my thoughts. The camp was in darkness, without fire or any sounds of humans. I was the first to put my head into a makeshift lodge, hastily cut from saplings and covered with cedar boughs. And then I saw them—two adults and two children, their lifeless, frozen bodies lying cuddled together, wrapped in a blanket of rabbit skins.

I turned and motioned my father to leave this place. We did not take the time to wonder of their fate.

Running, running. Late into the night we were running in complete darkness, the sky covered with a blanket of thick clouds, a new moon. We ran down a deep ravine and to the top of a rise. Then we could hear them. Wolves.

What shall we do, I sent my thoughts.

Be still, the answer. So we lay motionless under some balsam saplings, breathing hard from running, our fur wet and steaming. And we knew now we had probably already been discovered.

Then almost suddenly, they were there in front of us, two males and their mates and a juvenile.

The alpha male spoke. What tribe are you? This is our land.

My father spoke for us. We are the descendants of the wolves of Turtle Island, the island of islands, the sacred place, the place of secrets. We are descendents of the great wolf *Ogema*, my son's namesake, he said, who led the rebellion of wolves with the arrival of the new man-wolves. And we are the descendants of the she-wolf *Waubun Anung*, alpha mate of *Ogema*, who was the first wolf slaughtered by the new man-wolves. We are on a journey and request safe passage through your land. We mean no harm.

The alpha male spoke again. Why should we believe your story? How do we know you have not come here to feast upon our bounty, to steal our mates? You know as well the fate of wolves like you who run without the pack, dare to infringe upon other's hunting lands.

And all the while the other wolf was speaking, my father was secretly sending his thoughts to me. Prepare to run. When I motion you to do so, run like you have never run before. Run hard and do not look back, even though your lungs are burning and feel like they will burst.

Then just as suddenly, he motioned and we were off. His speed amazed me. And I was hard on his tail, the other wolves chasing just behind me. Running hard, harder than I have ever run. Not looking back. My lungs burning, burning, running for what seemed like an eternity. My father sending his thoughts to me, run hard. Run hard. Think of the boy. Put his face in your thoughts, only the boy. Now run toward your thoughts.

And I did. I ran toward my thoughts, ran until the wolves tired of the chase, until we reached the outer fringe of their land, until the soft light of dawn began creeping over the earth. And then we ran some more.

Then finally, beyond exhaustion, we stopped. Too tired to find food, we both fell into a hard sleep. To sleep and dream of the chase, of running.

We slept briefly. We're almost there, my father spoke his thoughts to me. Then we were up, sore and aching, and off again. Running, running in full daylight, we were close, running.

Off in the distance now, we could see the bottom of the big lake, the great hills that mark its beginning, and the sacred mountain of our Ojibwe brethren. Running, running. We trod the thin ice across a river, past the island of spirits the Ojibwe speak of in their prophecies. To the boy whose scent I could discern, who I knew was alive, who I sent out my thoughts to, I am coming to you. I am almost there.

There were several encampments along the ridge of the mountain and we silently walked along the fringes of each one looking for the boy and his family. There were fires at some of them, but others were dark and cold and spoke of death. We did this while the sun moved across the lake and warmed the land.

The boy's scent was stronger now. Put his face in front of you, my father reminded me. Run toward your thoughts.

And I did.

Again, we came to an encampment, and this time I knew we had found him. I ran at full gait toward a makeshift shelter, around a dwindling campfire.

And there he was, the boy.

I jumped on him and licked his face, wagging my tail so hard my whole body was shaking back and forth, back and forth, the dog in me. The boy hugged me and spoke my name.

My father stood back at the opening of the shelter, composed, the wolf.

The joy in our meeting seemed to go on for the longest time and when it was over my father sent his thoughts to me. The boy, he said, his father is dead. And his mother, she is dying. And the boy is cold and hungry.

He again sent his thoughts to me. I will stay here with the boy. You secure us some food. And I did as he requested, leaving, even though I did not want to put the boy out of my sight. I went in search of food.

In my life I have become convinced there are times when the Creator walks right alongside us, and that day was certainly one of them, for my hunt was successful and a rabbit soon offered itself to me, which I brought back and laid in front of the boy.

We stayed in that place for days, my father and I taking turns with the hunt, for rabbits, mice hiding under the snow, voles and salamanders that lived in the stumps and the hollows of logs. We were rewarded as well with small birds, a woodchuck hiding deep in some deadfall. We stayed as the boy gained strength. We stayed while he buried his father and mother in the proper way, while he kept a mourning fire, and said the songs and prayers for the dead, and mourned for them for four days as was their custom. We stayed at a distance from his encampment during these proceedings, as was our teaching. For neither wolves nor dogs have any business with the ceremonies of our human owners. We have our own prayers and songs, our own ways.

And then, when all was done, we took him home.

The boy. My *'way ay*, the young Ojibwe boy who raised me, who became my alpha, who named me *Ogema*, without even knowing the name was part of my ancestry. Who saw something in me as a young pup. Who saw that maybe I was bigger and stronger than my brothers or sister, that maybe because I had my way with my mother's milk before they did, maybe because I comfortably took on the look and demeanor of my father.

The wolf.

A Bear Story

I know that a lot of people think I am just an old man who doesn't know anything and isn't useful anymore, and few seem to care about what I'm thinking or have to say, or care what will become of me. I know that. I can feel it when I talk to most people, as it is in the sound of their voices and the look in their eyes. I mean, I am just this old bachelor who lives in a trailer house out on a dead-end road on the fringe of the reservation and I don't get too many visitors except for a sister and niece and a couple of old fart friends, so not that many people really know me. And I don't have any of the cultural knowledge that so many of the young people seem to want from the "elders," as they call us now. I can't speak the tongue, although when I was a young boy I remember Old Grandma, that was all she spoke around us, and she was always speaking it to my mother and sometimes to my father as well, although she rarely spoke directly to him, only through my mother. So I grew up around the language, sort of, whenever I was home from St. Mary's School in Odana, anyway, that boarding school we were sent to, where all us young Indians were sent back then. So the language is not something that is foreign to my ears. It's just that I can't speak it, except for the basics.

"*Boozhoo. Aaniin*" (hello). That's about it.

So nowadays, with everyone going back to the culture and all, I'm one of those who are out of the loop, of sorts. I don't know much about singing them Indian songs they sing at the pow-wows. Never could carry a tune except when I had a few drinks in me, and then I could sing a Hank Williams song pretty good. Spent more time at the bar in the old bowling alley in Red Cliff listening to the jukebox than I ever spent at any pow-wow. Nor could I teach anyone to dance Indian. Got two left feet. Always have. At the pow-wows when they ask us elders to dance I go out there, of course, but my stepping is always a few beats off. And I never made maple syrup, so I can't teach anyone that, either. If anyone would ever ask I'd have to admit I like Mrs. Butterworth's better than anything on my cakes.

I used to make wild rice when I was a kid. All of us did then, for school clothes mostly. My dad, of course, always drank most of the proceeds from selling the rice, but we usually got a few pairs of jeans and shirts from our ricing money. I quit ricing fifty some years ago after I moved to the Cities, and when I came back here to the reservation thirty or so years ago the last thing on my mind was picking up ricing again. Nowadays the tribal council gives it to us elders, so who needs to do all the work of harvesting the rice anyway? Nor can I make or mend nets, or set them, so I'm worthless with fish as well. If I want fish I go down to the Pier Restaurant on Friday nights for the all-you-can-eat trout and whitefish special.

I don't know any of the legends, either, so I'll never be a storyteller. I suppose if I knew any I'd be in demand all over Ojibwe country. We had all of that beat out of us by those nuns at St. Mary's when we was kids. About the only thing I'm good at is cutting wood. Hand me a chainsaw and you'll see a craftsman at work. I can drop a tree on a dime.

I think nowadays when people look at me they just see an old man who doesn't know shit.

Anyway, a couple of months ago I got a firewood permit at the tribal council office that gave me the okay to harvest all the dead and down alongside the roads anywhere on the reservation, so I'd been doing just that. And I was up in Big Sand Bay because there was a big blow there a couple of summers ago and all kinds of trees got knocked down and the area needed cleaning up, so I had loaded up my saw, chain oil, and some mixed gas and drove out there in my old pickup, figuring on getting a load of nice dry wood to cut up and sell to the campers in Little Sand Bay campground. I was cutting up a storm and all covered with chips and smelling like chain oil and gasoline and getting hungry for one of my sandwiches all at the same time. And then I saw them bears, four of them.

I see critters all the time. Wolves, coyotes, eagles, fox, otters, you name it. Now even turkeys, for Chrissakes. Even saw a cougar once when I was walking the trail between Big and Little Sand Bays, although no one believed me when I told them. They said I must have been *gi-wasquaybe* (drunk). Bears I see all the time, though, so it's not like they are rare or anything. And I often see the same animals as well. All of us are creatures of habit, you know. We all have our places we travel to and from, our favorite paths, our haunts. Animals have schedules just like people.

I've been feeding a coyote visitor all season and he comes down the road by my place near every week to get his fill of scraps.

Anyway, I was cutting firewood at Big Sand Bay that day and I seen them bears, a sow and three yearlings, that's the first time I ever seen them before. That sow gave me a look and cut across the road and headed down over the ridge across Sand River, and then they disappeared into the brush on the other side and I figured that was that.

Well, that wasn't that, because a couple of days later while on my way to the elder center for lunch I saw them same bears again by the old dump off Blueberry Road, and they looked like they were headed to town, too. So I slowed down and honked at them and that old sow just stared at me like "who the hell do you think you are" and I rolled down the passenger window and yelled at them that they'd better go into hiding soon 'cause the white guys bear hunting season will be soon and they'll end up on the back of a flatbed with their tongues hanging out. I was thinking as I pulled away from them that maybe next time I should bring my rifle with in case I see them again so I might fire above their heads in hopes of making them afraid of gunfire so they learn enough common sense not to get killed. I'm not one to understand why white folks go hunting bears, anyway. I've always been opposed to killing anything for "sport," as they call it. Killing a bear by baiting it with rotten chicken guts and then siccin' dogs on it isn't my idea of sport. One thing I learned early on as a kid was that you don't go killing anything unless it's going to end up in your kettle.

Anyway, I hadn't seen them again for a couple of weeks and the bear season was in high gear, and one Sunday I was headed down Blueberry Road on my way to the restaurant at Legendary Waters Casino to meet up with some of my old friends for the buffet breakfast. I remember it was really foggy that day and when I rounded the curve where Blueberry meets Frog Bay Road the fog got really thick and I had to slow down to almost a crawl. Then out of the fog I saw them bears again, and they were walking down the side of the road, and then they disappeared into the fog, and appeared again up ahead of me. By then I just watched for them because I didn't want to run any of them over.

That last time they disappeared in the fog and I kept driving at a crawl watching for them. Then the fog cleared again. And instead of four bears there appeared four people, an old lady and three of her grandkids, two girls and a boy. They were dressed like old-time Indians, you know, like when I was a kid. The old lady was all in black, with the thick black stockings and black-laced boots and a long black dress. And the kids were in bib overalls and flannel shirts and their hair was all mussed up like they'd been sleeping in the weeds. I swear to God.

I almost shit my pants.

And of course, normally I would have stopped and offered anyone walking to town a ride, but no way in hell was I going to do that. Instead I hit the gas and that old pickup blew out a big puff of blue smoke, and I got the hell out of there as quick as I could. And by the time I got to the casino parking lot, I was just starting to settle down enough to think about what had just happened. There was no way I was going to share what just happened with my friends. If they didn't believe my cougar story they would never, ever buy this one.

On the Sundays I meet up with my friends at the buffet, we usually make it an all-morning event. Everyone has stories to share. We all grew up here and have known each other our entire lives, so there is plenty to talk about. I suppose the waitstaff gets sick of us because we sit there and blab for hours and don't tip, and a couple of us chew so we bring our own cans in and that must really creep them out. And I imagine the casino management would much rather have us out on the floor playing the machines.

Anyway, that day we were sitting there for a couple of hours with me pretending I didn't see what I saw on my way there, and then they came in, that old lady and three young ones. Except now they weren't dressed in old-time clothes but looking usual, like everyone else. If I had taken drugs when I was young, which I didn't, I'd have sworn I was having flashbacks, or whatever they are called, but I wasn't. This was about as real as it gets.

They got a table on the other side of the restaurant and from then on I couldn't listen to a word any of my friends were saying because all I could think about was what I saw back on the road, and was happening again just across the room. And I watched as each of them, the old lady and little ones, loaded plate after plate of sausages and bacon, and blueberry pancakes, like they were starving and hadn't eaten in months. I swear to God they ate like bears, they did. No talking, just chewing hard and breathing through their noses. Then when they were done they all got up at once and left, and I overheard the waitress say the old lady left her a fat tip.

After they left I asked my friends, "Hey, you ever seen that old lady or kids before?"

But no one had.

I took the main road home that day, avoiding Blueberry Road like it carried the plague. And the next time I went cutting wood up in Big Sand Bay I brought the dog along for company. Like my old dog could stop four bears from tearing me up and scattering me all over the road. Like they would do that anyway. What I really tried to do, though, was pretend what I had seen that Sunday really wasn't what I saw. That what actually happened was it was foggy that day and the bears wandered off into the woods and there really was an old lady and her grandkids a few steps ahead of them, who just happened to be there as well. I think sometimes we need to hear that rational voice in order for us to move on in life. Like life is rational.

I DON'T HAVE MUCH for family left, a sister who had a couple of worthless kids, she emphasizes, except they gave her several wonderful grandchildren. Sometimes when she comes out to visit me she brings one of them along, a girl twelve years of age. The girl, *Andonis* (meaning "my daughter"), was given an Ojibwe name by her worthless father, who disappeared long ago from her life, but left her with a hauntingly beautiful name. And *Andonis* is always so kind to me and calls me Uncle. Often when she comes out with my sister she brings the awards she has won in school for her work, as well the newspaper clippings of the powwow news which list her among the winners in the fancy shawl category, whatever that is.

"Look, Uncle," she always is beaming, "look at these."

She is always so proud and even though I don't know much about what she is talking about, I am truly proud of her. Proud that she is doing well. Proud that there is a little girl somewhere in this world who loves her uncle enough to want to show him how well she is doing. And always before she takes leave from one of their visits she gives me a hug and tells me she loves me, and to take care of myself, and that she will be out to see me soon. And I who have always been uncomfortable with hugs always melt.

Sometimes when she leaves I am almost jealous of my sister that she has such a wonderful granddaughter. And often I even feel regret because I have lived the entirety of my life without a life partner, without children and grand-children to call my own. That in all inevitability I will die alone without anyone holding my hand and walking me down that final, long road as far as they can.

Anyway, last weekend my sister and niece came out to visit and sometime during the visit my niece made mention of seeing an elderly lady and three young ones walking down a side road just up the road from my place. My sister said she didn't see them. And my heart jumped then, surprised more than anything. Confirmation maybe that I wasn't crazy, that what I saw that couple of Sundays past was real.

"I saw them," *Andonis* said. "The elder woman waved back to me when I waved to her."

Later when we all went for a walk, I asked her to show me where she had seen the four, and although I would never tell my sister or niece, I saw fresh bear tracks where she said they had been.

Anyway, after they left that day, I worked up my courage and took the dog and my walking stick and went back to the spot where my niece had seen the old lady and three young ones and began following their trail. Not that I am any kind of tracker or anything. Far from that, I sometimes think I could get lost going out to my outhouse and back. The bear tracks led up the tote road about a quarter mile or so, then veered off into the bush, a trail of sorts that I followed. Sometimes curiosity gets the better of us, I suppose, and my grandmother would have said that curiosity killed the cat. I hoped not. Into the bush for about another quarter mile or so, and then to an open field, and in the middle of the field was a small tarpaper shack. And I don't know what suddenly gave me the courage to do so, because I remember being completely chickenshit for most of my life, but I went to the door and knocked. The dog stayed back at the edge of the field, whimpering.

The old lady opened the door, and said, *"Boozho. Aaniin. Umbe. Bein di gayn. Na mi dubin."* (Hello, come in and sit down.)

And I did, even though the only thing I could understand was the hello part.

Even though my old heart was beating about as hard as it could without giving out, I stayed and visited with the old woman and her grandkids. And as old as I get I will never forget my grandmother's teaching that we shouldn't stare, but that was a hard rule to follow that day because I couldn't help but look all around the small, one-room cabin. For hanging from the rafters and off all of the walls were dried plants and roots of all shapes and sizes, and a corner table and counter were covered with mason jars filled with various teas and liquids of all sorts.

"My medicines," the old woman said, who I now knew as *Zozed* (Susan). And we left it at that because although my mind was filled with unanswered questions, my demeanor is not to question because another of my grandmother's teachings reminded me that to do so would be most impolite. She was kind and her grandchildren, although very quiet, were as well. She offered tea and I accepted. We exchanged conversation.

"I live down the way a half-mile or so."

"We just moved here."

I wanted to know from where but didn't ask. "I think I saw you at the casino buffet breakfast a few weeks ago."

"Yes, we were there."

"Was that you walking down Blueberry that day?"

Not a reply, just a twinkle in her eyes and the hint of a smile. We switched to weather. "It was really foggy that day."

"It's going to be winter soon. I suppose we'll have to move in to town then," she said.

Soon it would be getting dark, and I knew it was time to leave. One of the children came to me and gave me a small beaded item. A gift.

"What is it?" The young one just smiled and stood there.

"A wood tick," the old woman said, "a beaded wood tick. Hang it from the rearview mirror of your pickup. It'll look nice there."

"I'd like to visit with you again."

"You are always welcome here."

So for the next several weeks I went often to their little shack in the middle of the field to visit *Zozed* and her grandkids, all who seemed to live in the old way without the conveniences of electricity or running water or government food commodities. I never did ask her last name. In fact, I was almost afraid to ask for fear it really might be Bear. And I who am an old man felt like a child in her presence, this woman who was so old her face was as smooth as a baby's, whose bluish-black eyes probably needed cataract surgery, who spoke to her grandchildren in the tongue. And I have to admit that my curiosity did get the best of me because I couldn't help but ask questions about all the plants and roots hanging about their little home, and she would go from plant to plant and to the different teas and tell me what it was, or what it was made of, and its uses.

"Maybe next spring when I come back I'll take you out when I do my gathering and you can learn right along with my grandkids," she said.

"I am just an old man," I said, "too old to learn anything new. I'll probably forget as soon as you tell me." But I knew in my heart this old lady was many, many years my senior, and her mind was quick and sharp, and she remembered.

I think the approach of winter announced itself with all my aching joints speaking loudly at the same time, almost screaming snow and cold. When I awoke one morning I thought I'd go visit the old lady one last time before she moved in to town for the winter.

"I have a daughter who lives in Duluth so we'll go there for winter," she had said. So after my morning oatmeal I started the walk to her place, bringing them a gift of some maple sugar cakes I'd gotten some months ago at the tribal council's elder dinner. I hardly got out of the driveway when I could heard the voices. Laughing, swearing, some dogs barking—hunters, just down the road toward the lake, not far from my place. Then I could see them clearly and they had a bear spread out in the bed of a pickup. And I don't know what possessed me to do what I did. I almost ran down the road to where they were, and I don't remember exactly what was coming from my mouth as I did but I'm sure it wasn't morning niceties. "You get the hell off out of here," I remember saying. "This is Indian land. You don't have any business here." And as I got closer to their truck I prayed it was not one of my bears. *Not one of my bears,* I was thinking. And those white guys just looked at me like I was crazy.

Then I turned and walked as fast as I could up the road and down the tote road and through the bush to the field, to the little shack. And by then I was out of breath and almost in a panic. The door opened and the old lady was there, and once inside I saw they were all safe.

"What's wrong," she asked, and I had to lie and say everything was fine, and I was so relieved I could have hugged them. So that day I know I overstayed my welcome, I just didn't want it to end, for I knew I might not ever see them again, because when you're old you never take the coming winter for granted.

"We'll be back in the spring. We will see you again. You come here again in April and we'll be here. You'll see."

WINTER WAS LONG and cold and there was plenty of snow. There were many times my road went unplowed for days while the trucks busied themselves in other, more settled parts of the reservation. And we all know that in winter it gets dark early, and stays dark for what seems like forever, and that we awaken in the morning and sit for hours before first light. I've spent so much of my life alone like that, it seems. And with each season the winters seem to have gotten longer, and darker. Loneliness sets in. My old friends seem to do the same thing I do and stick close to home so I don't see much of them either, except once a week or so when I make the drive in to the village to do lunch at elderly nutrition. And my sister and niece, maybe I see them once a month if I'm lucky, although it seems to be almost a lifetime between their visits. My sister is getting old as well and doesn't like driving much in the winter, and *Andonis* is busy with volleyball, basketball, and who knows what else. So when they do visit I cherish the time I have with them.

"Why don't you come and live with us in the winter?" my sister sometimes asks.

"I miss you, Uncle." *Andonis* follows. "You can have my room."

I beg them off for I have old habits and ways and also cherish the quiet and being alone. I have the birds and deer to feed. They would starve without me. And don't forget the neighborhood coyote. I would not know how to live without my privacy, not even without the loneliness that goes along with it. For even loneliness becomes like an old friend.

So the days pass and winter has its way with me. I busy myself feeding my animal neighbors. Days are spent out in the shed tinkering with things where I build up the fire in the barrel stove to keep warm and burn all of the garbage and scrap wood, and the cedar and balsam that can't be burned in the house stove. There I sit in an Adirondack chair I made from a kit many years ago and whittle and make things from basswood. I talk to the dog and he flops his tail on the dirt floor of the shed, lying next to the stove for warmth, and I scratch his belly. In the afternoon I make a ritual out of walking the half-mile up the road to the mailbox to collect my mail, mostly grocery circulars and junk mail trying to sell me Medicare supplemental insurance, and when I return home I take a nap. I always cook dinner and set out the table the way it should be, with my napkin on the left with a fork, and spoon and knife to the right of the plate. My evenings are spent reading and working on puzzles. Sometimes I pick up the old guitar that sits in the corner gathering dust and try to tune it up, even though it needs a new set of strings, and sing out of tune some old song I use to know, making up words along the way. I am almost always in bed by nine.

And I dream of spring.

Winter passes.

By mid-April most of the snow has melted, except the piles along the ditches left by the plows, and I'm on my way to town to get dog and bird food, more deer pellets, a new flannel shirt, and to meet up for lunch at the casino with the friends who have survived winter. And as I bump along on Blueberry near where it junctions with Raspberry Road and the old Pageant Grounds, where the old-time Indians use to dance for the tourists in the summer nearly one hundred years ago, I see the sow bear standing away near a cleave of woods and open field. And I bring the truck to a stop and roll down the window and speak to her as she walks, moving away from me at an angle into the woods.

"Boozhoo. Aaniin." All of the Indian I know. "Hello, my friend. I missed you all winter. It's good to see you again. I'll come see you soon if it is okay." Then I pull away as the bear disappears into the old-growth cedar and yellow birch.

I visit and have lunch with my friends and stop at the hardware and feed and grocery stores, then stop at my sister's for a haircut. The day passes quickly, and it's getting dark before I finally make my way home.

The next morning I take the walk to the old shack. Wood smoke is coming from the blue metal chimney protruding from the roof so I know she is home. I knock. And when the old lady answers and invites me in I notice right away she is alone.

"Your grandkids?" I ask.

"Oh, they stayed in Duluth with their mother. She's sober now, and she got cable TV and the Internet, and they have this Play Station. An old lady like me can't compete with that."

And I say, "But they will still come and visit you often, I bet, they'll miss their grandma," and she just smiles slightly as she makes her way to pour us some coffee.

We visit often now, all spring and summer and into fall, my new friend. And as promised, she has been teaching me all about her medicines, one by one. We go far out in the woods sometimes to gather.

"Put that tobacco down before you gather. And leave some of the plants there to grow and multiply, always. Don't take it all."

There are the ones gathered early in the spring, before the new shoots. There are ones gathered from new shoots. There are the roots harvested during each of the three seasons. The leaves. Flowers. You dry some. Boil some into a tea. Pound some into a poultice. Mix some together.

"Bitterroot is good for sore throats. You chew it like this."

"This squirrel tail you chew and put on a cut. It will stop bleeding."

"Brew swamp tea for colds."

"Strawberry root, you boil it and put it on skin eruptions."

"Resin from this tree you grind into a powder and put on sores."

"Roots from wild celery will cure tuberculosis."

"These flowers from the boneset you pick just before the first frost and make into a tea and it will stop a fever."

"For heart trouble you use sturgeon potatoes, gathered in the fall."

"Bear root and catnip, you mix them for fainting and when one's heartbeat is weak."

My new hobby, I call myself the plant guy nowadays. And I know so little about my culture I don't even realize what I am learning, that this is ancient knowledge, that I am becoming a keeper of the bear medicines. That I should thank the old lady for her gift of this knowledge, that I should bring her tobacco and offer it to her for this knowledge. So now my old trailer house looks like the old lady's shack, with jars of teas and roots, and plants tied together drying and hanging from the ceilings and on shelves.

And then one day in late fall when I go to visit her, to learn more about the plants, she tells me she will be leaving soon.

"I'm going to go live with my daughter now. I miss my grandkids too much. They got cable TV and I like that Old Country Buffet."

She's laughing and so am I, but my heart is breaking at the same time, my friend and teacher, my elder, the bear woman.

"I need to know so much more," I say. "You're the only one who can teach me." But she says that I only need to pray and ask the Creator from now on, and all of that knowledge will come to me.

THE SNOW CAME EARLY this year, bringing its quiet hush over the land. And I settled into my winter pattern as I have done for all of these years.

Then one day my sister comes to my door. "*Andonis* has taken ill," she says. "You need to come into town to see her. She's asking for you."

"What's wrong?" I ask.

"She has some kind of fever, so I took her to public health. They say she has auto immune, maybe from a tick or something this past summer."

"Wait here," I say. "I need to get my medicines."

ANDONIS RECOVERED FULLY, of course. I knew she would. And even though I can't speak the tongue, I still had my medicines, and I prayed over her in the only language I know. Then when she felt better I gave her that beaded wood tick, the one given to me by one of the young bears.

Boozhoo. Aaniin, Creator. *Daga* . . . (please). I learned a new word, it says a lot, goes a long way.

I know that a lot of people think I am just an old man who doesn't know anything and isn't useful anymore, and few seem to care about what I'm thinking or have to say or care what will become of me. I know that. I can feel it when I talk to most people as it is in the sound of their voices and look in their eyes. I mean, I am just this old bachelor who lives in a trailer house out on a dead-end road on the fringe of the reservation, and I don't get too many visitors except for a sister and niece and a couple of old fart friends, so not that many people really know me. And I don't have a lot of the cultural knowledge that so many of the young people seem to want from the "elders," as they call us now.

But I have that bear knowledge and know them plants. And I'm teaching it to my niece so it will carry on.

Acknowledgements

Wolf story from Benton-Banai, p. 8

Made in the USA
Monee, IL
20 July 2021